The Moment of Movement

THE MOMENT OF MOVEMENT
Dance Improvisation

Lynne Anne Blom and L. Tarin Chaplin

UNIVERSITY OF PITTSBURGH PRESS

Published by the University of Pittsburgh Press, Pittsburgh, Pa., 15260
Copyright © 1988, University of Pittsburgh Press
All rights reserved
Feffer and Simons, Inc., London
Manufactured in the United States of America

Library of Congress Cataloging-in-Publication Data

Blom, Lynne Anne, 1942–
   The moment of movement.

   Includes index.
   1. Improvisation in dance.   2. Movement education.
I. Chaplin, L. Tarin.   II. Title.
GV1781.2.B57   1988   793.3′2   88-1332
ISBN 0-8229-3586-4
ISBN 0-8229-5405-2 (pbk.)

To Aric, my son, who cried, "Oh no, not another book!" **L.A.B.**

and to my three, Daniel, Tamara, and Scott, whose moments are full of movement. **L.T.C.**

Contents

Introduction

Improvisation, which has always been a part of folk and theatrical dance, became more visible in the artistic community in the 1960s with postmodern dance, particularly in the work of Steve Paxton, Yvonne Rainer, Trisha Brown, and Anna Halprin. Its therapeutic value has brought it to the attention of psychotherapists, and lately it has even found a social niche, in gatherings for Contact Improvisation. This attention has resulted in a renewed interest in, and respectability for, improvisation in the academic setting.

Little has been written about improv,[1] in part because it is so elusive. Not only is it ephemeral, but at best an improv is a constantly changing phenomenon. Trying to pinpoint in words exactly what dance improv is seems at times to betray the medium itself, for language is linear and improv is not. What is very real and understandable in movement does not necessarily have an equivalent in words. Aldous Huxley talks about this danger when warning of reverse alchemy. We touch gold, he says, and it turns to lead; touch the pure lyrics of experience, and they turn into verbal equivalents of tripe and hogwash. Nevertheless, it is our belief that a lot can be said about improv—clearly, concretely, and without romanticizing.

The Moment of Movement provides basic information about how and why dance improvisation works. Its concerns are both theoretical and practical. We discuss the role of movement as medium, the elements of the creative process, ideas for creating improvs or adapting existing ones; but we also answer the questions of beginners and provide a checklist for successful leadership. Because it would be pointless to offer the ideas without examples, the final chapter of the book contains suggestions and ideas for over two hundred improvs.

This book is for everyone interested in dance improv. There are no

[1]We will use *improv* as a shortened form of *improvisation.*

secrets that only the leader should know. As a matter of fact, discussion of the concepts basic to improv can deepen awareness more rapidly by going right to the heart of the matter and address cognitive issues that may unconsciously be preventing or limiting certain actualizations. This book is also for the person interested in improv in other mediums or in the creative process in general, or for those interested in the aesthetic, abstract, or theoretical aspects of dance, irrespective of any specific interest in improv, for in exploring the latter we shed light on the former.

In *The Intimate Act of Choreography* we wrote that "dance improvisation fuses creation with execution. The dancer simultaneously originates and performs movement without preplanning. It is thus *creative movement of the moment.* [It] is a way of tapping the stream of the subconscious without intellectual censorship, allowing spontaneous and simultaneous exploring, creating, and performing" (p. 6). Improvisation in movement is analogous to free association in thought, which is "the most spontaneous, primitive, natural and creative process."[2] The kinesthetic self is free to partner the imagination impulsively, without preparation or preconception. Improv implies a lack of contraints, a diversity of possibilities to follow in any direction for as long as the mover pleases. It exists outside everyday life, creating its own time-space boundaries, seeking only its own inherent profit and goal. In ordinary life we learn to distinguish the real from the unreal; in play and improv we acknowledge all realities. Make-believe becomes as real as gravity and equally, or more, potent.

Artists often speak of trusting their intuition to guide them, or even more radically of becoming a channel through which the vast creative forces of the universe can speak. The creative act thus takes on a life of its own. By becoming the instrument rather than its master, we gain access to broader realms. The impulses spew and spiral at will, seemingly of their own accord. They become plentiful, then overabundant. There comes a time when we need to be willing to gather those impulses and to tame them. It is in the taming that

---

[2]Lawrence Kubie, *Neurotic Distortion of the Creative Process* (Kansas City: Noonday Press, 1958), p. 55.

intricacies begin to appear and additional possibilities are seen. Taming is the role that Apollo plays in balancing the passionate, intuitive, intoxicated Dionysus; it is necessary lest the intensity lead to chaos and avoid forming, which is the ultimate satisfaction and completion of the creative act. Although it is intoxicating to ride the power of the impulse, the act of shaping gives even greater strength to the unleashed creative forces.

Improvisation is the dynamic daughter of dance, at times self-indulgent, at times concise and determined, but always developing and changing. She has a free spirit; she should be given free rein within wisely and flexibly set boundaries.

Note: Since movers and leaders come in both sexes, we use the pronouns "he" and "she" interchangeably.

All improvs, set in **boldface** type, are listed in the index.

Acknowledgments

We would like to express our sincere appreciation to the following people: Lynda Martha for her ideas and enthusiasm in reading a very early draft; Penny Campbell for taking time from her improvising to carefully review the manuscript and make suggestions; Bonnie Morrissey, Susan Lee, Ben Blom, and Deborah Miles for advice on selected chapters; and Catherine Marshall, our editor, for her keen eye and staunch support of those who write about dance. We would also like to acknowledge the institutions that we have been associated with during the writing of this book and have lent their support in a variety of ways: Northwestern University, Middlebury College, Jerusalem Rubin Academy of Music and Dance, and Penn State University. And finally we thank our students, our living encyclopedia, for without them there would be no book.

The Moment of Movement

1 Movement, the Foundation of Dance Improvisation

The varieties of human movement are legion: reflexes, gestures, accommodating maneuvers, posturings, precise complex articulations, random actions, and practical and aesthetic patterns. Sometimes movements are displayed openly (a hug or a salute); sometimes they are hidden or so minimal as to be only internally identifiable (a jumping inside your stomach). All of them can be, and have been, analyzed in terms of space, time, and energy. Together these elements differentiate one movement from another and give each a unique identity. Depending on the nature of the movement one element may predominate, but the others always contribute by supporting and refining the movement: in finger tapping, the primary time element is augmented by the direct use of confined space and a light degree of energy.

Movement is both expressive and practical. It contributes to, and mirrors, human growth and development. As instinctive forces, intuitions, rhythms, and passions drive us, our bodies respond to unspoken needs and desires, interpreting the continuous flow of internal and external signals and determining the appropriate form of action. The neuromuscular system—muscle contraction, nerve stimulation, touch sensation, adrenaline formation, muscle fatigue, oxygen depletion—provides a parallel flow of feedback along with our sensitivities to gravity, pressure, breath, tension, and verticality. Our comprehensive body intelligence apprehends other realities (walls, stairs, moving bodies) and adjusts the movement accordingly.

Athletes and dancers commonly carry movement to extremes. Excessive activity produces various results, depending on the type of movement engaged in. Breaking sweat, a simple and tangible phenomenon, creates an immediate awareness of the body; this affirmation of the self-alive-in-the-body creates a hunger for more movement. The physiochemical high engenders a psychological high; together they make a potent brew, yielding a rarified perception of self. The monotony of excessive repetition, however, produces quite a different result, leading as it often does to a deepening hypnotic focus. Movement-induced dizziness, a third form of physical excessiveness, changes the sense of body boundaries and can cause calm transcendence or nausea.

At times we are frustrated by our body's limits, for they hinder our heart's fantasy; yet at other times we surpass those very limitations, reaching places and creating events we never dared dream of. Such physical limit-pushing (as with getting past momentary exhaustion and into a second wind) brings an exhilaration that reaches well beyond the physical accomplishment alone. In a dance improv, the movers may achieve the exhilaration that comes from challenging physical limits, but because they are pursuing something beyond the physical, they have the added gratification of spontaneously creating unique movement and form.

In investigating movement specifically as the medium for improv, there are three things to consider: the kinetic-kinesthetic event, the instrument (the particular dancer), and the form. Movement acquires rhythm and articulation as a result of gravity, momentum, speed, and phrasing. Moreover, one movement may demand the next—one must return to the ground after a leap, right oneself after a daring off-balance movement, or come to a dead stop after multiple fast turns. As a kinetic-kinesthetic event, the movement is sensed, experienced, and perceived physically.

Secondly, movement in improv is inextricably part of the instrument itself, that is, of the particular dancer: her body type, self image, personal affinities, movement style, and aesthetic choices. The whole person defines the instrument; accumulated experiences, values, tastes, and desires all qualify how the body will respond. Technique also plays a role here, for it primes the body's skills, strengths, and weaknesses in practiced patterns and integrates them into a coordinated response system. Technique also limits through selective avoidances. Certain movements are perceived as awkward, ugly, uninteresting, or impossible, and they are programed out of the response system. With all its complexities and nuances, each dancer's body is a unique expressive instrument.

The third aspect is the form, that which emerges from the dictates of a developing structure. The mover makes choices that conform to, or realize, an overall form. This can be seen as an *intention to* or *orientation toward,* form, which may be the communication of an emotion or a dramatic idea or simply an expression of the beauty of form itself—the gathering momentum, the climax, and the recapitulation. Human beings have an innate drive to give form to experience. For often form is the *communiqué entier:* it is simply about itself. Movement becomes the subject matter, completely self-sufficient. (See the discussion of Abstracting and the Abstract in the next chapter.)

While these three concerns supplement and support each other, one is often the primary determining factor of a given movement or movement series.

MOVEMENT AS COMMUNICATION

Current literature abounds with references to the power and informational value of nonverbal communication. From formal studies of the kineticists and our own observations of daily life, to novels and theatrical performances, we are constantly impressed with the ability of the body to support or contradict verbal declarations. It has been estimated that 70 percent of daily communication takes place on a nonverbal level. Except on the telephone, verbal communication occurs within a nonverbal framework that is an intricate part of the message.[1] We have all known the difficulty and frustration of trying to convey a powerful experience through words alone. Communication involving aesthetic or emotional experiences can be greatly augmented by physical input, especially when it is a spontaneous telling. A skilled writer or poet weaves in a sense of the physical.

Situations from daily human interaction have parallels in improv:

[1]Desmond Morris's *Manwatching: A Field Guide to Human Behavior* (New York: Abrams, 1979) is an extensive and fascinating resource book on nonverbal communication. Another, particularly valuable for its coverage of the major systems and theories, is *Inside Intuition: What We Know About Nonverbal Communication* by Flora Davis (New York: New American Library, 1975).

in daily life	in dance improv
The listener moves in time to the speaker's speech pattern (which signals paying attention).	The less assertive person of a duet accommodates in movement to the more assertive partner.
Shared opinions result in shared postures or movement qualities.	The performer mirrors or shadows movement or shares its quality or basic design (i.e., curves).
A group takes on a shape reflecting the status and relationship of its members.	If participants are equal, a circle or undefined mass will form; if there is a leader, it will be shown by distinctions of space, time, or energy.

Improv capitalizes on the communicative aspect of movement when other people (co-movers and/or watchers) will respond to the universal that is being expressed. For example, I can understand and connect with your movement about fear even though my experience of fear may be of failing, or falling, while yours is of an abusive father. I am able to move with you, and I identify with your improv or dance because the fear has been reduced to its essentials, to its movement, to the primitive state that is real in all of us. This common base forms a river of truth of the human experience because we know things for their dynamic and kinesthetic truths as well as for their intention or specific references. Realization through movement allows such truths to be abstracted, not away from their emotions, but away from their specific triggers. Movement is the connecting thread that allows me to join you in movement, dance the fear, and let you know that I too know about it, have been there and am here now with you. It is the same knowledge that lets me and a hundred thousand others see Martha Graham's *Errand into the Maze* forty years after it was created and say, "I know."

THE CREATIVE PROCESS

Although the medium of dance improvisation is movement and that movement has meaning, what of the phenomenon itself? What of, as a philosopher might ask, the "aboutness" of improvisation? Can it be explained and defined? Can we unravel or even probe its essence, its generic identity? Certainly and easily we can say that spontaneity is one of its constituent parts. At the same time it is not without direction. It is at once intentional and reactive, causal and accommodating. An organic strategy or plan emerges to take us forward in time, yet it only becomes articulated as we move. Because improv is a phenomenological process, we cannot examine any product per se. But it does exist and it is perceivable. What we can do is examine the route it takes (and our consciousness of it), a route which is on the way to creating itself while being itself.

Creativity, simply defined, is *bringing something new into being.* What is new can vary from something new for the individual, to something new for the culture and time, to something uniquely new. *New* may also be defined or qualified by context, or by the grouping or attitude that surrounds it. That is because movement, ideas, and people do not exist in isolation; they work in combination, as catalysts for one another.

Rollo May, in *The Courage to Create*, says that creative people "give birth to some new reality, . . . express *being* itself, . . . [and] enlarge human consciousness. . . . Their creativity is the most basic manifestation of a man or woman fulfilling his or her own being in the world."[2] The creative process has four major stages: (1) preparation; (2) exploration; (3) illumination; (4) formation or formulation. The preparatory stage includes exposure to the basic ingredients of the art or science and development of the skills it requires. During this stage the specific problem is stated and researched, and a background is established. The second stage, exploration, involves a letting go, a giving up of conscious control, allowing many options to be tried, explored, and experimented with. Creative thinkers agree that the sometimes hard, sometimes enjoyable, and often lengthy period of exploration is usually followed by a time of laying the problem aside, consciously or subconsciously. The issue is thus given time to bathe in the recesses of the intuitive where the ideas roll around and regroup. It is a receptive yet not a passive time. Attention is placed elsewhere while the main issue is purposefully put out of mind. (Some creativity

[2]Rollo May, *The Courage to Create* (New York: Norton, 1975), pp. 39–40.

analysts see this latent period as a stage unto itself.) From out of this dark place, most often unbeckoned, comes a flash of insight. It is the "Aha!" moment or illumination stage. Things come together; the plan is seen, the theory clear, the image articulate. The potential of the new idea is apparent. During this breakthrough, everything becomes suddenly vivid; there is a heightened consciousness in which the sensory, memory, and thinking processes are intensified. The fourth and final stage involves giving outward form to the inner image. The forming or formulation which is developed in this stage is necessary for the objectification and articulation of the image or solution. This will allow the clarity necessary for its communication.

What is essential to all the stages is an encounter and a willingness to engage in intense involvement. The encounter commingles the material, the creator's preconscious, and the external world, and has a vitality as well as a validity of its own.

CREATIVITY IN IMPROV

The nature of the creative process is basically the same for many different kinds of endeavors—the making of a poem, the formulation of a scientific theory, or the creation of a dance—but what may take place over a number of years for a scientist or a choreographer may happen in minutes in an improv. It is tricky to ascertain how the four stages manifest themselves in a single improv—that is, assuming that they all do. Some improvs are almost exclusively exploratory, with the movers forever trying this and that and yet going or culminating nowhere; and then there are others in which a creative spark occurs almost immediately with little or no priming or experimentation. But even in a creatively successful and well-formed improv, do all the stages happen in sequence? or simultaneously? Is the "Aha!" that governs or tempers the exploration and the forming process immediate or suspended?

I am a scientist, I fall asleep and dream of a snake eating its own tail. Aha! I immediately understand the nature of the solution I have been looking for.

The snake metaphor led the scientist to the immediate understanding of his problem; there was an instantaneous "Aha!" While the working out of the formula or its ramifications may take years, *the understanding arrived full blown.*

In improv, the "Aha!" often occurs simultaneously with the instructions, the first three notes of the music, or the first phrase of movement response. But at other times the recognition and understanding come during the course of the improv; you are "Aaaahhhaaaing!" or "Oh yesssing!" *while you are moving.* This is because a dance takes place in time—it cannot be completely perceived by the performer or the observer in one instant, like a painting. So the recognition comes with the *moving "Aha!"* rather than all at once.

The evolving "Aha!" brings both a sense of the whole (the form) and a clarification of the intention. Specifics become clear in the doing.

> While I was improvising I sensed some intention evolving. I didn't see it all in one second; I only recognized it *as* I was moving. If I'd been stopped in the middle, I wouldn't have the whole shape because it was still in the process of becoming.

Sometimes the "Aha!" becomes conscious only after the improv is finished, maybe even days later. In these cases it most likely will come as an immediate and holistic, rather than as a suspended, "Aha!"

Although we can speculate about how and when the various stages of the creative process occur in improv, it is far too whimsical and unpredictable an event to follow any predetermined plan, logical or not. However, in leading improvs one can structure the input and instructions in such a way as to foster access to each of the four stages. (For ideas on guiding structure while leading, see chapter 8, "Create Your Own Improv.")

These different stages of the creative process are more or less present in all kinds of creative acts, but it has long been acknowledged that while the process remains the same, the types of creativity vary. There is a qualitative difference. The formulation of a major scientific theory or the creation of a masterful work of art differs significantly from the creativity we find in children's play or in laying out a garden. But whatever the type, all creative activities share a fundamental element: a very particular kind of consciousness which we can specify as *creative consciousness*. There are three basic ways of perceiving and responding: focused consciousness, diffused awareness, and creative consciousness. Focused consciousness is rational, logical, yang, verbal, manipulative. Diffused awareness is receptive, yin, nonverbal, and accommodating. Creative consciousness, however, is intensely attentive to the matter at hand while being attuned to all possible relevant associations, no matter how far afield, tangential, or metaphorical. It combines an attention to the surrounding field and shifting intentions at the same time as it retains the ability to capitalize on those elements in order to focus and craft.[3] Creative consciousness may be an alternate way of referring to the experience which, in ritual and performance, is known around the world as "possession." Graphic artists and scientists, as well as performers, talk about *being one with* their material, about the moment (or moments) when the person becomes inseparable from the process and the product. Dancers may be one with the music, the character, the spirits, or the movement.

At first, creative consciousness listens to the rumbling of the material and refrains from editorial or censorial decision. It thrives on the rich activity. Later it allows crafting skills to come into play. Curiously enough, even the crafting is intuitive in nature.

In speaking about their own experience with creative consciousness, movers have tried to give verbal expression to their experiences:

Often it feels like you are holding your breath, afraid to label, to even look with conscious critical eyes, for the flow may stop. It is a delicate vigilance, difficult, like trying not to blink. It is a mixture of patience and a desire to get in there and run with the momentum.

Sometimes I ache from refraining, I ache from holding the gate-

[3]These distinctions are made by Jean Shinoda Bolen in *Goddesses in Everywoman: A New Psychology of Women* (New York: Harper & Row, 1984). She uses *Aphrodite consciousness* where we use *creative consciousness*. See pp. 226–29.

way open, allowing the preconscious, the intuitive, and the reflexes to mingle with my experiences and my skill in crafting. I am suspending intervention of the critical but at the same time overseeing and making sure that things are happening, that I am not just moving around, that I am allowing, responding, and crafting. I suspend conscious control because I know there is no way I can consciously carry out all the things I am doing naturally.

In this state of delicate balance, movements are refined as they flow out, elaborations are embroidered, and inappropriate distractions simply evaporate rather than being coldly censored. This passive objectivity is possible because, as involved as we become in movement, we can retain the capacity to simultaneously be the silent witness who assimilates, synthesizes, sees. As this capacity grows (and it is one of the root skills which is gained through experience in improv), it provides feedback that is objective without necessarily being judgmental. The crafter can be encouraged without inhibiting the rush of movement and ideas. It observes while impregnating that intuitive rush with valid, pertinent perceptions, challenges, or considerations and questions.

The exploratory crafting skill must always be tempered by the knowledge that it humbly serves the creative process and must not control the reins to the extent that it would allow the observer to flip over to the searchlight of linear thinking. At times, it seems we are a perpetual mediator between the demands of passion and those of the critical, crafting sensibility, between indulgence in sensation and the urgency for form and order.

ASSOCIATIONS AND CORE IMAGERY

As we have seen, an improv can be just about the movement, but at other times the movement can call forth associations in the form of ideas, memories, or images which become the core of the improv. These can be as intangible as being swept up in an energy force flowing in figure eights around the room, and as suddenly realized as an unintentional intention ("I seemed to be pulling everything toward me") or as concrete as a found task. Even when our concentration is totaly absorbed in the pure aspects of movement, a sense of something can come unbidden. For example, while concentrating on being light and fast, we sense that we are whirling endlessly in the far reaches of outer space. The specifics of the movement provide the trigger: light and fast calls forth a different image from strong and fast.

Sometimes, as we move, related actions or metaphors become possible and relevant. For instance, as you experiment with linear paths going in and out from your body, you begin pulling at your clothes, letting them snap or sag back, changing your body shape, rearranging yourself inside the clothing, taking some pieces off, adding others. Or an image can remain purely spatial, having design, volume, and even movement of its own. It can be a fantastical thing partnering you in unexpected ways or an architectural maze of delightful shapes and hiding places. At still other times the core image is revealed simply by its strategy, its plan. We understand it by what it causes us to do.

When the core is a specific image we may actually see it in our mind's eye. A mental image is a complex sensory experience perceived in the absence of that which it represents. Although we hold it mentally, it may be kinesthetic, visual, auditory, olfactory, or gustatory in nature. In dance improv the most prevalent kind of image is kinesthetic or kinesthetic mixed with visual. If it is visual, it may be quite specifically representational or it may be a more abstract image which conveys its essence in a sensual, holistic, or gut way with few details. For example, in an improv that I perceive to be about my relation to my father, I sense his presence and related connotations and memories but I may or may not actually see a visual image of him. There may be only one moment when the movement actually calls up a mental-visual image of him. Some people can't conceive of dance improv without images while others see images only occasionally or not at all.

As we move, one awareness leads to another. Memories arise and fresh associations trigger new material. How this works varies with the improv and with the people involved. An image does not have to be about one thing; it can jump through time and space and be peopled with characters of changing identities. The layering may bring an influx of details, or a rich array of distinct but separate images. A movement can cause a vivid sensation that in turn feeds a detailed image that in turn fuels further movement and new sensations. Movements, sensations, and images slip and slide against each other, gaining richness and value in the process. Sometimes the images spring spontaneously from the movement, but sometimes they are specifically directed or implied by the instructions. (Using images as a basis for creating instructions is extensively explored in chapter 8, "Create Your Own Improv.")

Besides the movement of the present moment, one of the major contributors to the core image can be kinesthetic memory. A kinesthetic memory flares in our moving muscles; triggered by a movement we are doing, it recalls other times or movements. For example, as we rock we remember other rockings. Muscles remember childhood experiences, learned dances, shifting a car, and one-time improvs. Sometimes when an improv is over you can't remember any details, but in time it may flood back, as a dream does. The memory is caught in the preconscious, in the sensing organs, and in the muscles. A particularly strenuous, sensuous, or dangerous movement flares into awareness.

This phenomenon, known as muscle memory, allows memory, images, and meaning to be encoded in our muscles. Reports of this are common throughout the literature; people who have been "Rolfed" (a slang reference to the body work of Ida Rolf) speak of having images or past events pour forth during deep tissue manipulation. The process also works in reverse, from images to muscles; as we imagine lines of action along anatomically and kinesiologically correct paths we can, without moving, cause changes in our muscles. Such processes underlie the theories of Lulu Sweigard. Dancers use a variation of this when rehearsing mentally. Some of the work done in various healing modes depends, at least in part, on using such imaging to produce desired change. The work goes both ways, image to muscle and muscle to image, causing deep connections.

Remembering an improv is not necessarily seeing or being able to recreate a specific series of positions or movements. Rather it is often the context, strategy, relationship, intention, or a real or imagined environment that comes to mind. Other times it is only a remembered sensation with no sense of direction, shape, or theme. Each improv has its own epithet.

Memory of an improv experience of sixteen years ago is still felt in my kinesthetic system: the intensity of the unique movement style (I took on someone else's very rapid, high energy, intense movement), the encoded plan (to ease him out of the place that he seemed locked into and bring him to one of sustained, liquid movement), his face and expression (fear, then trust and joy) and a sense of the two of us seen from another's point of view (our leader's), my feelings of oneness with him and of accomplishment.

MULTIPLE INTELLIGENCES

Kinesthetic memory is but one example of a truth that artists and athletes have known for years, but that academics have just begun to give credence to, namely, that there are multiple intelligences, including the linguistic, musical, logical-mathematical, spatial, bodily-kinesthetic, and intra- or interpersonal. Most recently Howard Gardner, a Harvard psychologist, has brought new focus to this theory in his book *Frames of Mind*.[4] A number of these intelligences come into play in dance improvisation. They are not minor systems, or information-gathering centers, that serve the so-called higher verbal intelligences. (There are no "higher" systems, only ones more appropriate for a given task.) Rather they are valid systems of knowledge that stand on their own with no need for verbal aspects. Each is its own reason for being and differs qualitatively (in terms of its essential nature and therefore of its use), rather than quantitatively, from the others. Often the knowledge contained in the system cannot be translated into words; in fact, words may cloud or warp the understanding, execution, or communication of that knowledge.

Einstein said that "the words of the language, as they are written and spoken, do not seem to play any role in my mechanisms of thought. The psychical entities which seem to serve as elements in thought are certain signs and more or less clear images which can be voluntarily reproduced or combined.... The above mentioned elements are, in my case, of visual and some of muscular type."[5] Such a

---

[4]Howard Gardner, *Frames of Mind: The Theory of Multiple Intelligences* (New York: Basic Books, 1983).
[5]Ibid., p. 190.

process is thus actually an independent mode of thought and is one of the natural ways research scientists, artists, and others hold or even discover concepts. Its power is further recognized in fields including psychology, medicine, meditation, kinesiology, and politics. The arts and sciences (math, chemistry, and physics in particular) represent huge fields of human endeavor which are elementally grounded in nonverbal systems. These nonverbal or alternative literacies have substantial bodies of knowledge in and of themselves. It is important for us to realize what this experiential body of knowledge is and how it functions within the realm of movement in order to gain a deeper knowledge of improv.

2 The Experiential Body of Knowledge

Some things that we know with great certainty cannot be communicated to anyone else—except by striking the proper piano key or offering up the ripe avocado for the tasting. Words fail, and without benefit of the experience itself, the would-be learner remains in total ignorance. The reason is as simple as it is frustrating: the senses are not verbal. We could say they are a-verbal, being neither pre- nor post-verbal. Movement improv, being an activity related to the senses, is also a-verbal, and the knowledge it carries can therefore only be learned and known through experience.

Direct experience builds a fund of tacit knowledge which becomes embedded in the body's response system. Responses mix with perceptions, building on each other to form a complex system of knowing. Besides kinesthetic responses, there are sensations, psychological awareness and agendas, mental images, and kinetic phenomena. The resultant accumulation is integrated into each person's response system to form a unique experiential body of knowledge. Such understanding is intuitive so that by the time an underlying concept is verbalized (as in a discussion or in this book), you say, "Ah, yes, I know that." The verbalization reinforces your knowledge and extends it from the intuitive to the conscious level. Thus the act of improvisation, together with discussions or readings, all build a fuller understanding of improv useful for participation as well as for leading and creating improvs.

Through deliberate structuring, the more basic improv experiences will form a foundation for others. Some of these progressions take place over a session or two, others over a term, while still others mature over a lifetime. The different experiences and concepts provide a web of continuity as each builds within itself while feeding the others. Beginning with tentative exploration and tender, even non-dancey (yet necessary) first steps, a clear progression brings the mover to confident, formed, creative movement.

When we first become involved in movement, make choices, and tentatively form the experience, we are learning—if you will—to function creatively in movement. As we become more involved, experienced, and responsive, we increase the possibilities of having more unique things happen because our resource pool and our tools for fashioning and utilizing those resources have grown. Our responses become freer, shelving the analytical censor and liberating the subconscious, so that the explorative self can increasingly engage in physical experimentation. Soon there are more and more moments of intense involvement, allowing the creative process in each succeeding improv to become more active.

Accumulated experience results in better-educated hunches. A series of successful experiences allows a novel one to be approached and pursued with greater confidence; such success yields a willingness to risk, thus building a vivacious cycle of positive feedback.

In order to achieve this desirable cycle, the mover must be truly involved. We must be willing to take risks, committed to the experience, and ready to be vulnerable and open to the self-discovery that is a natural product of the process. We must also be willing to listen to others and to be generous with them. An active balance of self-fulfillment and response to others' needs has to be maintained. Basically we need the courage of our own impulses and responses qualified only by a healthy concern for the people we are working with.

Each of the following contributes to the experiential body of knowledge: kinesthetic awareness, phrasing, forming, relating, and abstracting.

KINESTHETIC AWARENESS

Kinesthetic awareness should be an automatic result of a well-guided improv. Beginning improvs that are sensory in nature help develop this primary perception.

What does it feel like to fall and rebound, to roll, to touch and be touched, to support and be supported? Can your elbow press, tap, or rub other parts of your body? How does that feel? What's the difference in sensation between making large slow circles with your arms and making tiny, fast ones? Or the difference between snapping your fingers rhythmically, with the rest of your body stoic as stone, and snapping your fingers while tapping your feet, rolling your head, and undulating your body all at the same time? What is the range of an isolated part of your body? How heavy is your head? Can you feel the cohesiveness of the whole body moving with one intense focus, all parts collectively contributing? When is your leg really straight? Where is center? How far off from it can you go before falling? How does gravity influence your movements?

The answers to these questions are not found in words but in one's body, in the awareness of the experience itself. As that awareness grows through repetition and experience, bringing increasingly more sensitive and immediate feedback, the ability to produce and direct movement with greater subtlety and range also increases.

The body knows many things and can learn many more as various knowledge systems work together. Self-awareness depends heavily on the proprioceptive (or "perceiving of self") system by which the body judges spatial parameters, distances, sizes; monitors the positions of the parts of the body; and stores information about laterality, gravity, verticality, balance, tensions, movement dynamics, and so forth. The body has its own sense of timing, geared to getting something done accurately and efficiently. It coordinates the reflexes, finds and automatically integrates the rhythm, tempo, and sequence of events to allow the movement to flow forth as easily and naturally as possible. The body knows when to change direction abruptly, not just in response to actual physical danger but in accordance with the requirements of design, or phrasing, or to pursue a specific idea. The body knows, without conscious pre-assessment, how fast you need to run and when to take off so you can leap against the wall, rebound easily, and land safely, all the while looking ahead to accommodate the next movement. It also knows how to accommodate itself to someone lifting and manipulating it; it is ready to adjust with the right position and body tone. (Contact improv provides a fine example of this.) The body can perform many actions you would never attempt if you constantly stopped to consider one set of circumstances after another. "All of a sudden I realized I had leapt over her. I had no idea how I did it." Dancers may struggle to master certain complex movement skills, but there are many things the body knows and can do without such training.

When carefully conceived and well guided, an improv course builds a repertory of movement. There is no need to pretend that an exciting, innovative improv has all "new" movement in it, or for that matter, *any* new movement. What is new is the realization by the dancer. Uniqueness is created by the combination of movements, the context, and the consciousness on the part of the mover.

PHRASING

All movement contains innate rhythms and phrases which provide the magic ingredient in any of the performing arts. In viewing the accomplished dancer we often praise her musicality, but it is not musicality alone that underlies an exquisite sense of timing. While master choreographers wed music and movement, a sense of timing and phrasing exists even when there is no music; the body simply responds to its own knowledge of movement linkage and organization. It knows how movements belong together and creates phrases without being consciously directed to do so. The quality and the subtlety of this knowledge increase with movement experience and can be cultivated through guided improvs.

Movements will naturally tend to collect around an impulse, a breath, or an intention, with relevant material forming a self-contained unit or phrase. A movement starts, goes somewhere, and ends; another idea starts, thereby invoking a new set of movements, a new phrase. Phrases will vary in length and shape according to the content: for example, a hand flutters around the face coming quickly to rest on the opposite shoulder; a wild series of runs and leaps circles the room many times before finally coming to rest curled in the corner, on the floor. Both are phrases; each is felt as a single complete unit.

Since phrasing usually occurs naturally during an improv, it should occasionally be brought to the forefront of the mover's attention to see how the movements group together and form distinct units. Does the end of one phrase introduce or suggest the next, or does the new one erupt with an altogether different direction and energy? Both possibilities will and should occur, for life and forms sometimes follow linear and logical patterns and other times impulsive, irrational, and even random ones. These patterns may be conscious or intuitive in their physical realization.

FORMING

Most of the time when an improv works you can look back and see the form. Sometimes it is clearly built into the instructions ("start little, get bigger and travel, then return") or into the image (a life cycle). But form can also result from the ongoing impetus of the movement itself. Just as we tend to move in phrases, we also tend to group them—to explore a subject, take it somewhere, and resolve it. Human beings are forming creatures; we like to organize, create sets, form gestalts. Form alone, in and of itself, can be the main focus of an improv. But its strong and obvious potential also lies in its ability to organize pure movement (so that it is not a mere collection of steps) and to support and clarify images and dramatic intentions. Form crystallizes content.

With or without a specific image, movement builds on its own necessity, its own impetuousness, its own desire to seek form. Form is produced in the ongoing immediate, yet seeks a final overall structure as well. This larger or complete form satisfies and justifies each individual moment and in turn leads unerringly and inevitably (though possibly with much elaboration and complexity) to the end.

Forming is an unfolding, evolving process which supports yet also responds to the ongoing movement. Form is being spun into existence as phrases of movement pour out and directions are taken. A sense of order hovers; as movement accumulates it creates a framework which determines new movement. So while a specific end is not inevitable, ensuing movements are influenced by what has already happened. We sense the direction of the phrases; we find ourselves making choices that seem consistent with the forming pattern. As we continue, the form solidifies; there is clarity and at times great complexity.

In realizing an overall form we use transitions; they may be imperceptible or stunning and neon lit, according to the demands of the piece. The momentum (physical or dramatic) often creates its own transitions. There can be an abrupt change from low level to high ("get up and run"), a gradual transformation ("you want desperately to get up, but it is very hard"), or a rapid alternation until the new material takes over ("roll on the floor, occasionally let the roll take you to your knees, continue to roll and rise alternately, building the rising until it takes you to standing").

Our tendency to create form profits from our ability to see patterns, not only simultaneously occurring ones (as in a painting) but in a series that progresses over time. As we move we discern the pattern forming: approach/leave, approach/tease/leave, approach/touch/leave, approach/intertwine/leave, approach/conflict/leave. The pattern provides the internal structure while an overall form is created. From the four seasons to a fugue, from natural patterns to complex mathematical, musical, or movement ones, we find satisfaction in making and seeing patterns. We see sculptural shapes and our place within them; we extend, balance, or counterbalance the design as well as the dynamics of the moving group. Combined with a sense of rhythm, this patterning ability instructs us to pass through a fast-moving group or join a structure of bodies, being sensitive to the various lines of force, balance, and composition.

Form supports the intent and content, forcing decisions. It needs to be fulfilled yet it also needs time for relevant tangents. But the form drives; properly honed, it generates a forward motion toward unity and wholeness.

The tendency to form may appear only sporadically in a beginner's improv until it is acknowledged and valued. Sometimes the dynamic shape of an improv is crystal clear (and often completely unnoticed by the mover); at other times there is an undistinguished gray smudge of unformed movement. This tends to happen when the movers are not involved and are producing movement without a focus, or simply for a desired effect. It can also happen when they are honestly involved but no value has been placed on the act of forming or on the discipline to see things through. Then they jump enthusiastically from one movement idea to another, dropping unfinished work in pursuit of a new adventure. As forming is fully cultivated and becomes automatic you may want to experiment and build improvs around aborting the realization of form. (See chapter 9, "Advanced Challenges.")

RELATING

Dancing alone is wonderful, but humans are social animals; we like to be with and relate to others. Group improv is a social form; it fosters processes similar to the ones a child goes through in growing up. This process of becoming socialized is developmental, with each step depending on the previous one.

The first requirement is to develop a sense of self and become comfortable with that self. An emerging being, whether it be an infant or a beginning student, has as his first interest exploring his own physicality, sensations, and emotions. In improv there are numerous ways to introduce and reinforce a knowledge of and security with the self. On an introductory level there is kinesthetic feedback (moving, touching, and being touched), isolation of different parts of the body, and an awareness of emotional responses and personal imagery. Later on there is one's personal movement style, which reflects the hues and gambits of personality, training, idiosyncracies, values, preferences, and so forth.

Once a comfortable and heightened sense of the moving self is achieved, the next step, relating to others, follows. From a secure home base, you can seek another person to move with. Not only is this satisfying in itself, but it generates confidence, new movement experiences, and a deepening trust in interpersonal interaction which in turn provides new positive feedback about one's own sense of self.

Improv extends beyond ordinary social interaction since it breaks many of the culturally determined taboos about body boundaries and personal space. Contact of all sorts (eye, touch, feelings, ideas) is encouraged and developed. With increased exposure and experience we become more comfortable with psychological and physical interaction. As our level of skill rises we are led to ever greater experimentation.

Whether we are moving with people or just observing, we participate in their movements. We pulse with their rhythms and thereby know on a deep level about the delight, calm, or frustration they are experiencing. This is kinesthetic empathy. It takes us from seeing another person's movement, to knowing of it and responding to it. It allows us to take on someone else's movement, feelings, visions, to identify with him in the shared experience of movement. Through empathy we reach a common point from which we can engage or counter the other.

A common example of this is imitation. It is the art of the mime, the comedian, and at times the therapist, and it is a natural, even automatic, response pattern of children, friends, and lovers. It is a way of learning, bonding, and communicating. Imitation is an integral mechanism in improv. Sometimes we slip into the skin of the person or people we are working with by taking on their movement styles and thereby their attitudes. Although our own movements may differ in detail, we adopt their flow and use of space, their tempo, rhythms, and weight, their kind of responses and style. We integrate their way of moving into ours and consequently begin to know them better. As we interact, the mimic mode usually does not predominate; rather, the tendency is to slip in and out of it. Sometimes we take a single aspect of our partner's movement and develop it, taking her with us. Think about daily conversations where you get caught up in your friend's animated humor, depression, or gentle givingness. You try it out, keep what you want or need, and let the rest slip away. When you take on another's movement you do not lose yourself. On the contrary, you enable yourself to exploit resources that may have been hidden, untapped. This is as exciting and enriching an aspect of partnering in improv as it is in friendship.

Once we have broken through the cultural barriers and gained some experience in working with others, group improv offers lots of new movement opportunities. You can jointly create designs, actions, and rhythms not possible with one body. If you are working with a partner you can follow his lead, responsive yet resting in his authority. You may carry or lift parts of each other, dragging, molding, and sculpturing. Or you can have an argument with movements flying like sparks, complementary but not of one mind, competitive yet unified by the joint intentions of convincing the other. In response to your attention your partner grows, opens up, or closes, revealing himself in movement; he feels safe, or threatened, and finds new movement to express that; he takes risks and gains confidence with his new-found skill of communicating physically. Ideally this is reciprocated and each of you touches deeper within, accepting the other, celebrating similarities and differences.

A group improv imposes a different kind of relating than that found in one-to-one work; it is less personal, and, in a sense, less flexible. What you give up in freedom you gain in the exhilaration of unity. For some, group improv is an acquired taste because it necessitates a shift in attitude, but it soon becomes a new addiction. A group improv takes on a life of its own as individual responses jell. To accomplish this the priorities of the individual change from "this movement feels good to me" to "this movement is right for the group as a whole." The needs, directions, and energy of the new and larger entity take precedence, and the resulting movement must create, define, and maintain it. For example, the group has been moving in a circle and gradually something starts in the center which is different from the energy on the periphery: it is less aggressive, less rhythmic, more supportive and serene. This poses two compelling possibilities: either join the new structure growing in the center or maintain the rhythmic vigilance around the edge. If the improv's identity is accepted as being about the circle and its center, then going off to a corner and floating by yourself would detract from its cohesiveness. There may, however, be a time when such a response, even under the circumstances just described, is warranted: if the center group began a floating motif, you might perceive that as a nesting image and become a solo figure venturing away from the home base yet belonging to it. The point is that the movement is conceived in relation to the continuously evolving identity of the group.

As cohesive as a group of people improvising together is, their spontaneous groupings and encounters can reveal an amazing amount of diversity. As you watch groups moving together you will see various patterns of relationships emerging, basic ones often supporting a variety of energies and intentions. Some of the things that happen are reminiscent of games or folk dances.

As no two individuals are alike, no two groups are alike. The nature of the group is determined by its size (a quartet cannot create the same entity as a group of fifty-five), as well as the age, sex, and personalities of its members. A group of six-year-olds will of physical necessity create a different spatial, sculptural, and temperamental environment than a mixed group of adults and children. The degree of trust, level of experience, and length of association will all affect the degree of intimacy, abstraction, and subtlety.

ABSTRACTING AND THE ABSTRACT

Abstracting is a fairly automatic process in dance improv. As we translate concrete images to movement, we abstract; as we create movement metaphors for symbols and verbal instructions, we abstract; as we manipulate a motif designed from a gesture, we abstract. Eliminating the particulars makes the resultant movement closer to the universal experience that claims us all. Often we start with the literal and proceed to the abstract, a shrug of indifference becomes a floppy, throw-away dance. Other times we may start with the abstraction, adding specifics and zeroing in to the literal: a wild, running, jumping dance evokes the exuberance of winning the state championship, which in turn shifts to a miming replay of the last touchdown. Within one improv different degrees of abstraction are often mixed, a gesture and a swing blending comfortably.

People have affinities for different degrees of abstraction in art. The painters Andrew Wyeth and Jean Arp stand at opposite ends of the spectrum, as do the choreographers Martha Graham and Alwin Nikolais. This preference will also turn up in improv. Most beginners tend to be quite literal but with good guidance will come to appreciate the possibilities of abstraction. That is not to say that abstraction is a better or higher mode of improv cognition and production, just a different one.

In the process of abstracting we eliminate the particulars that tie us to everyday behaviors and responses. By manipulating the movement, embroidering and embellishing it, we find out more about it, nudging into the cracks, penetrating its core and seeing what indeed it is all about. How far will it stretch before it becomes something else? When are flickering movements no longer a candle; at what point do they slip into a furnace fire, transform into a moth, or deteriorate into unfocused, uncolored movement, movement without the soul of a candle?

Abstraction can lead us to essential truths, truths that emerge because the experience is not tied to practical considerations. "Of course I could never really carry my father, but I did in the improv, I cared for him, protected him: shouldered him as my responsibility; he wasn't a burden. Actually the weight [of responsibility] felt good; I felt good."

You are abstracting as you deal more and more with the essence of an experience, either where specifics do not intrude at all, or where there are a multitude of images and yet the essence is different than their sum. For instance, as the person you are moving with blocks your way, leads you around, pushes you down, encloses you; as he becomes a ticket taker, gatekeeper, policeman, parent, god, lion, teacher; as he goes beyond character and represents a trap, a prison, or the color black—the essence (in this case, of authority) becomes multidimensional. Images slip from one to another without concern for detail or logic.

Often images will mix; some fleetingly coloring the moment, others well explored.

> As I was playing with lightness and elevation I connected with joy, as freedom, buoyancy, a caring, a giving in. At times I was a child, having a child, racing toward a friend, laughing with a friend, romping with a puppy, holding a sleeping kitten, being a butterfly, then a bird, swooping, being the color blue, twirling so fast I dissipated, filling the room with joy.

Every medium offers its own means and access to abstraction. To abstract a tree into dance takes more translating steps than to abstract it into a painting. By contrast, abstracting a hug works easily in dance. In order to gain entry to the process of abstraction as it works in dance improv you might want to start with images that have a basis in movement: hugs, attacks, and falling, instead of trees, apples, and flowers. Of course what one chooses to identify as the essence can vary. For instance, is the essence of a flower its shape, its metaphorical function as a life symbol (the act of budding, blooming, and withering), or simply its beauty? The children in a creative movement class reach for the essence of blooming as they start with their heads covered and then uncurl. The ballets that depict a rose are able to abstract beauty because of the professional dancers' exquisite ability to transcend their very human bodies as they create a nonhuman movement ambience that bespeaks the essence of pure beauty itself. There are no "rose gestures" to use, and a rose pattern on a costume simply provides an elegant yet unessential accent to the theme.

At higher levels of abstraction, the medium itself becomes more pronounced and active, creating its own sense and syntax, its own magic. At times it may even take over and distract us from the image we were working with. Fascination with the medium (the physicality of movement) takes us to the purely abstract, a place without attitudes, stories, or assumptions. The purely abstract differs from even the most abstracted version of some concrete image or gesture. It refers to nothing and is self-sufficient. J. S. Bach, John Cage, George Balanchine, Jackson Pollack, Piet Mondrian, Alwin Nikolais, and Merce Cunningham are all abstractionists, pursuing lines, tones, designs, and movement for their own sake and for their inherent aesthetic appeal. They have no "meaning" but are important in and of themselves. These designs need not be suggestive; they may be striking, appealing, or even fun, but they are self-contained, independent of reference. From this independence they draw their beauty and their power, offering a logic and clarity not possible when referring to the reality of our human world. (See chapter 5, "Leaders' Concerns," for a fuller discussion of the abstract and the influences of perception.)

By working consciously with the above five aspects of dance improv we vastly augment our experiential body of knowledge. The results are beneficial to layman and professional alike: artistic awareness and perception, intellectual and intuitive understanding of movement and dance, expressive and creative ability within the medium, analytic skills vis-à-vis nonverbal aspects of communication. The concepts are not purely theoretical; they are physically achievable and therefore must be experienced in order to be fully known.

3 Beginners' Questions

W*hy are we doing this?*

People improvise for many reasons: to enjoy movement for its own sake (for its quality, rhythm, shape, and patterns); to warm up the body, energize it, and release tensions which come from inhibitions; to make personal, emotional, and psychological self-discoveries; to gain a fuller sense and use of the body; to explore another form of communication and expression; to be a part of a group, transcending self; to develop performance skills. To improvise is to dance without the pressure (and yet with the option) of imitating someone else's movement, style, ideas, or impulses. To improvise is to participate in the creative process and bring form to the impulses of the body and spirit.

I never took any dance classes so how can I do this?

You can improvise in dance even if you've never studied dance. Surprised? Many trained dancers find themselves frozen if they are not given specific steps with specific counts. This class starts from basic movement and develops improvisational skills. All you really need is the basic ability to move that you use all the time. From there, it's an open ball game—and therein the fun and the challenge. Improv is not about "dancing" in the theatrical sense of the word. It's not about how high you can kick, or how gracefully you move. The improv experience strives for access to movement nonjudgmentally—to the blunt and the grounded, the funny and the bizarre, the sensuous and the lyric, the wistful and the meditative. It actually devalues show, feat, and being pretty for prettiness' sake.

But I took lots of dance classes!

Of course you can improvise if you have had lots of technique; it is just different. You have to learn to *respond* in movement instead of learning given steps. For a little while you must let go of the codified, artificial vocabulary and reflexes of a dancer. Later, your technique will come to your aid; it will serve your images. Your strength and control will bring a precision and articulation to your vision. But for now, most likely you have to let go of "dance" as you know it.

Obviously the more finely tuned the body is, the more material there is to work with. The ideal is a highly trained dancer's body, responding to the free improvising spirit with a consciously crafting sensibility.

What is the ideal background?

While having improvised before in dancing, acting, or music may help, the important thing is the willingness to physically commit yourself to the movement, to take chances, to respond authentically to kinesthetic and sensory impulses, and to make a fool of yourself if need be. It can also be an advantage if you are used to working with images in your head and have an active fantasy life. Through improv you can pursue your imagination and the intuitive, impulsive forces of your subconscious while you develop your creative tools and sensitivity.

How does movement improvisation work?

Even before we take our first gulp of air, we move in the womb. Our most primitive responses are ones of movement. Our moving bodies both receive and give information about the world we are living in. The intricate feedback system that connects sensations, perceptions, and responses is made possible through the wonder of the body we too often take for granted. From cradle to grave it is our vessel, our medium for existence, experience, knowledge, and communication.

When movement is layered with awareness, perception, recall, and we are utilizing its integrating function, it is inherently satisfying because it is life affirming.

How do I know if my movement is right?

It can't be stressed enough that there is no single right way to move. If you are involved and responding honestly to the instructions as you understand them and not arbitrarily or insensitively interfering with anyone else, then "you are right." Unlike math there are no wrong answers, but innumerable right ones. Therefore, there's no point in checking what everyone else in the room is doing. Their responses may be right for them but wrong for you. In improv each person is at the helm of his own ship. Occasionally the fleet needs to unify or change its direction. Remain open and alert so you can respond appropriately when this occurs.

But what is the leader looking for?

The leader is looking to see if you are involved, in the movement and in the moment. Her experience enables her to see if the movement is inwardly evoked and connected. The movement may linger, play around the edges, or even repeat itself before it takes a new direction, but an ongoingness is evidenced. She watches for the thread that brings it from the beginning to the end.

She is looking for an honest response, minimal as it may be. She is checking for contrivance or self-conscious obviousness. Improv is not the time for showing, but for feeling, noticing, and pursuing.

She is looking for the hard-to-define quality known as *flow*, not in the specific sense of lyricism but in the sense of organic evolution. The movement can be (and often is) abrupt, even abrasive or discordant, but one movement should spring from another with an inner kinesthetic logic. The movements may be surly or surprising, having sudden tangents or contradictions, but these will be called for by the momentum or subject matter, and they define the flow and focus the intention.

All of this is what you will come to learn by being in the improv class.

Will I know when the movement is connected?

With time you will develop this sense. You will find a moment when you've become lost in the movement, the image, the form. It is a moment of complete involvement. Of course, you will move in and out of involvement—one moment you are involved and the next find yourself outside. The way to reconnect is by getting back to the movement. Improv is not always a religious experience with a guaranteed high; there are gentle and subtle connections to be cherished and nurtured. Involvements get deeper as you let them; you have to give in to get in.

Why should I close my eyes?

Working with your eyes closed aids in centering and concentration. It heightens the sensory and kinesthetic focus because it eliminates the element we do most of our perceiving through, the visual. It insulates and isolates you from conflicting stimuli, from other people's movement ideas which might in their uniqueness tempt you away from the integrity of your own. Closing your eyes may also help you to see images.

Obviously, when you charge around the space you'll need to see where you're going, for your own and everyone else's safety. Yet there is a way of keeping your eyes unfocused, allowing you to see a wall, a body, or an obstacle without its distracting details. Try keeping your eyes half-closed and unfocused, or use peripheral vision, focusing beyond or next to a person. When moving with someone you know, this technique can help to filter out distracting elements of your relationship.

What you don't need to do is check to see (1) if the leader is watching you; (2) how you look in the mirror; (3) what Sam is doing in the corner; or (4) if you are doing it right. Don't compare yourself with others; it doesn't work with these goals. When searching for honest, creative responses, there is no one to copy. If improv teaches you nothing else, it will urge you to look to and trust in yourself; it will support you in honoring yourself and the validity of your impulses.

Do I have to keep my eyes closed?

If you can move from your own center unselfconsciously and independently of others, fine, keep them open. Some people find the "closed eyes" approach too touchy-feely for them; others who have a strong dependence on visual orientation may actually find that closing their eyes limits their willingness to move freely. Experiment and find out what's best for you.

How do I begin?

Ideally you want to be centered, that is, responsive and ready. Listen to the instructions and then let your body try things; don't think about it first. Often, especially in the beginning, the movement will start slow and small, in an isolated part of the body, perhaps tentatively seeking to establish a connection, experimenting to find which movement, which part of the body, best responds to the stimulus. Conversely, the instructions or your own impulse may propel you to initiate the improv with a frantic burst. Your inner sense will be the judge. Trust it and know it will get smarter the more you use it.

But I can't dance—there's no music!

It is fun to dance to music. The rhythm gets and keeps you going, the overall structure gives you a direction, the melody gives you ideas of what to do. For these very reasons, it is best not to always use music in beginning improvisation. To put it another way, because music structures and dominates, you can become dependent on it. Consider letting the initial source come from the internal you, rather than the external music. This does not take away one iota from the joy of dancing to music; it just suggests a vast alternative. The beginning exposures to improv are usually developmental in nature and geared (among other things) to make you capable of improvising with or without music. Of course, you can hum or sing to yourself as you move, or you can perceive your movement as the singing of your body.

Man's body is also man's first musical instrument—clapping, stamping, and chanting. Music came from the body, so improvising first without music is a way of dealing with the two elements in their natural evolutionary sequence. With or without music, again and again, you'll find your natural movement will be exhibiting such musical elements as tempo, rhythm, accent, and phrasing.

How long do I wait for something to happen?

Be willing to wait one more breath. Try another part of the image. Go back to centering; eliminate outside and inside interference; give up self. Try even the smallest of movements to get started. Perhaps a sway or pulse, run or roll, will generate the physical momentum that connects you to the instructions.

What if I am not happy with what I am doing?

If you are uncomfortable or feel no connection to the movement you are doing, stop. Return to neutral and focus on another part of the instructions for motivation.

I had this great idea but I wasn't sure it would be allowed.

Trying out what you consider to be a great idea is precisely what *is* allowed and desirable. We are socially conditioned to follow orders literally, but in improv we must try to override that reflex. Improv aims to get beneath the veil of ordinary perceptions, to explore the extensive range of sensation, feeling, knowledge, and resources from which new constructs can emerge.

What do you mean when you say, "Let the movement take over"?

The movement has taken over when it has found its own direction, when it has its own reason and momentum, when you have given up conscious control, thinking ahead, deciding, and judging. With experience, you will develop skill in handling this slippery combination of relaxing, focusing, and giving in to what wants to happen. On different days you may need different ways of giving in to the movement. If you are uptight and harried, you may do it by relaxing; if you are scattered, you may need to focus in.

What if I am not using the improv idea that was presented?

Suppose, after you're already in motion, you realize you are not doing what you thought the improv was supposed to be about. First of all, remember that the instructions are a stimulus to get you going, so if you are going, don't worry. It is much easier for the leader to curb or redirect you than it is to break the inertia and get you started. Should the leader feel you have ventured too far afield, she can always unobtrusively pull you back in with a hint or indication. Otherwise, the choice remains yours: to continue to be faithful to what you have evolved and are involved in, or to drop it and pursue the common content. Of course, if you feel that your movement is not only disconnected with what was given but feels contrived, that would be cause for letting it go.

Also realize that in an improv with a rich bed of stimuli, many potential sources of movement will slip by you but serve as important hooks for your neighbor. It is a given that people will connect to different layers of a complex improv. If you take off on only one aspect of a certain stimulus, forget the rest; they may crop up later or not at all.

A half an hour? The improv seemed like five minutes!

Yes, being deeply involved in an improv can lead to a sense of timelessness. Our involvement allows us to ignore our cultural tendency to subdivide time into neat particles, accounting for each one. Time may seem to leap forward during an improv; on other occasions complete cycles and indeed lives run their course in a few minutes. It is one way to slip through a wrinkle in time.

Can I stop and ask you questions?

Once you get connected and start moving, keep moving. It is best not to stop and ask questions to clarify a point; go with what is working for you. Actually, an important part of improvising is making discoveries about the instructions *in the doing*. Trust yourself. Small details of the instructions are usually not essential to their implementation; they are there for enrichment.

The need to ask a question often cohabits with the old assumption that there is a *right answer*. Ask a question only if you are completely baffled by the leader's instructions. Then quietly, without interrupting others, go over to the leader and privately ask for clarification. Once you are responding, don't stop in order to listen to the next instruction; keep your own motion and connection to the previous image going so the new movement can evolve.

Sometimes you say, "Don't jump around, stay with a movement," and at other times you say, "Try something new."

These seemingly contradictory instructions are really one request—to find movement fresh and interesting enough to warrant your commitment.

In your attempt to be imaginative, don't seek out a collection of unrelated movements, trying one and quickly dismissing it to go on to another. Instead, consider each movement as a new territory to explore for a while. Stay with it; relish and repeat it; slow it down; speed it up; change its size, place, or focus. What is distinctive about it? Shape? Dynamic? Rhythm? Where can it lead?

On the other hand, don't get stuck with the same movement and fall into a rut. If you find yourself doing the same dance, using the same style or movement qualities over and over, then next time wait a little longer before starting. Try beginning with a part of your body you don't usually use. Change the rhythm or the energy. If you're lyric, try something jerky or rigid. If you're constantly drawn to twirls and being airborne, try working on the ground.

What do you mean, "Go next door"?

To find new movement, often it is easiest and best to start with what you are already doing and change one component at a time. You "go next door" not with radical changes, but with small gradual shifts away from your present movement. For example, you may be doing a small, easy, curving action with your hands, chest, and head and after a while feel a need for it to change. You let it grow in size; it gets large enough for the curve to cause a weight shift. Eventually you let the strength and the size of the impulsive curves make you travel. That traveling brings you "next door," to new movement.

What do you mean, "Involve your whole body"? Do I have to move everything at once?

No. Every part of the body does not have to move all the time. But having the whole body involved is having it be informed. The entire organism should know about the fingers wiggling even if the intention is complete isolation or indifference. Think of the nonmoving parts as being alert, in readiness. They're not idle, just waiting in the wings for their turn. The entire body can be significant, even when quiet: it may frame the movement by focusing attention toward it; it can resist in stoic defiance, thereby making a commentary on the mobile part. The point is that you are whole, not a collection of disparate parts. The connection is innate; we simply ask you to affirm that wholeness.

What do you mean by "Observe yourself as you move"?

Human beings can operate on different levels at the same time. For example, as we complete the last leg of a backpacking trip we: experience thirst and exhaustion, tie our child's shoe, and sense that the particular functional position we are in is sculpturally interesting. Such multilevel operations occur so frequently that we pay little attention and are not impressed. But it is this ability that the artist consciously cultivates.

After some experience in improvisation, when you've passed that awkward stage of self-consciousness, it is time to pursue the ability to stay fully involved while simultaneously observing your movement. It adds to the depth of the experience in several ways: it lets you have a sense of what you look like in movement; it facilitates group work by letting your antenna pick up on the process as a whole; it allows you to reflect about what is happening, thereby opening up opportunities to act on other options. You have probably already noticed this happening to you, since sometimes the instructions call for such awareness ("notice what parts of your body are touching the floor, which shape is curved, which angular"). Perhaps at some point you were particularly struck with some movement and tried to remember it. This objectivity comes and goes, depending on your needs and the workings of the moment. Although it occurs naturally, it's a sense that can be nurtured.

When do I stop?

The best answer is, when you are finished. However, the group leader will often initiate a conclusion by asking you to bring the movement to a close. How do you do this? In an involved improvisation, forming comes about naturally. There is a natural sense of phrasing: a movement starts, goes somewhere, and ends; an idea is moved and resolved, and another begins as the phrases keep rolling on. The end of a phrase is a good stopping point, so when you hear "Find a way to close," observe the next few phrases as you do them, allowing them to bring the larger momentum, the flow of the entire piece to an end. If there is dramatic intention, find a way for it to be resolved. Always take the time to find an ending that complements your personal journey; don't just stop because others have stopped.

Sometimes I get tired holding my last position waiting for everyone else to end.

Once you have established a definite closure you may relax and watch. When you are working with others, hold until you are sure it is over for everyone concerned and is not ready to start again. Sometimes there is a cadence but not a final closure, and the group, as with a single mind, begins again; be open to this option.

Why do we talk about the improvs afterward?

First of all, it is just plain interesting to hear what happened to the others in the group—in movement, in awareness, and in how they related to the instructions. Sharing feelings about what happened builds trust in yourself, creates a bond with the group, and strengthens the process in general. Discussions are an opportunity to translate a movement experience and your feelings about it into words and thus cultivate a more conscious awareness of the experience. Discussions also furnish a time to ask questions, especially silly ones. They furthermore provide the leader with feedback, a real necessity in the development of plans for continued work with the group. Sometimes, when a lot is going on in your head but there is only minimal movement, it is useful for the leader to know about it. There are limits to her ability to read the visual information you've provided or intuit the nonvisual activity that is so often an important part of the process. Also discussion provides opportunities to explain or share responses to others, to acknowledge or show appreciation, or to get objective feedback to your subjective experience.

What do you mean by "Did it work?"

This is one of those tricky phrases artists often use with complete authority and shared understanding but which is difficult to define. It means, among other things: Did the movement take over? Was there a good level of involvement? Did it feel honest? Was it fulfilling in some way? Did it satisfactorily confront and deal with the material? When an improv works, there is an intensity to the experience, the body and the senses form an intricate whole, a paranormal situation blooms.

When a group improv works there seems to be a little telepathy and precognition going on, like the sense of teamwork in group play. All involved sense the direction so things happen as if with one mind. One movement flows from another, the movement gestalt directing. This occurs not intellectually, or consciously, but intuitively. Things work smoothly, in a self-made order. The experience feels valid within its own created terrain.

Sometimes you say "Don't think." What do you mean by that?

It is a bad habit to repeatedly stop and try to think of something to do. Each such incident puts you in your head; improv is in your body. Start small and easy with whatever movement is happening, splendiferous or banal as it may be. For here the laws of physics are on our side; a body in motion tends to stay in motion.

Put your mind on the shelf; improv is not a cognitive activity. Respond directly in movement without filtering it through preconceptions and judgments. Thinking is inhibiting to movement, at times even incapacitating. If you've ever consciously tried to re-create the natural opposition of running whereby your right hand and left foot are forward while your left hand and right foot are back, you'll quickly understand this. Trust your reflexes and kinesthetic system, for they will guide you.

Wow! I just did some really weird things!

Yes, they were fantastic. Don't worry; be thankful. Your actions in an improv do not necessarily reveal your true self. Humans are multifaceted beings. While you need to own all that you do and take responsibility for it, you should not try to interpret or analyze everything. A character in an improv, like a character in a novel, owns its own truth, and as its creator you must allow its expression and not assume the world will believe it is your secret side showing.

Along the same line, don't take other people's crazy fun too seriously. A normally very gentle person might become a vivid, vile, insidious, schizophrenic adversary for a few moments when deeply involved in the dynamics of the movement. It is the movement that created this monster and this situation; enjoy it, or at least give yourself the chance to investigate and see it through.

Hey, that was funny! It was neat when he became a teasing clown. What did that look like? At first I worried that we shouldn't continue, but it felt like it really worked well.

It *was* very funny. You were all so serious, yet I could tell you knew how funny your movements looked. You really went for the unexpected response and cultivated a bizarre sense of character. There is always that opportunity for a great deal of richness in humor, so why not take advantage of it?

What if it had gotten silly?

Silliness presents greater difficulties because the improv tends to lose focus and deteriorate. Sometimes something can be silly and still work. Other times, it may not be that good as an improv but nevertheless serve an important auxiliary function for the social integration of the group.

But is it okay to laugh in a regular improv?

Yes. You can play, giggle, even laugh. Some movement is funny within itself or causes an association which triggers laughter. Let the laughter come but don't stop the movement: continue to pursue the improv. You might want to translate the laughter into movement so that the energy gets utilized. It may lead you to a new way of moving—rising swoops, explosive attacks, jerky or spastic trembling. If you are laughing from joy, surprise, or appreciation of an unusual situation, then it is part of the improv and let it be. Don't make more of the vocal participation than it deserves. If you are laughing out of self-consciousness and it gets in the way of your concentration, then it is inappropriate. If it is interrupting or violating the work of others, it is also inappropriate; move quietly to the side until it subsides. If it's really uncontrollable, use common sense and step outside the room. Laughing doesn't last long when you are by yourself.

Sometimes I want to cry.

Understand that improv is powerful; it binds together physical and emotional responses. If you hit this place, you're tapping some significant depths. If possible, allow yourself to allow it.

We really got tangled up. Is that okay?

Body contact is okay; it is part of improvising with other people. Introductory exercises purposely present structures using physical contact to get you to feel comfortable with various parts of the body touching and being touched, with supporting and being supported. These increase your awareness of body boundaries, of weight and gravity; they help you realize that the tactile mode is a communicative one.

The amount and quality of the contact will vary with different people and with the same people on different occasions. After all, people have strong feelings about the invasion of personal space, even when it's permitted by the rules of the game. Remember that you have a right to define your body space and act accordingly; you might invite one person in close while keeping another at arm's length. You are never obliged to be manhandled or imposed upon. The way you move and accommodate someone else's approach should alert them to your state of mind at that particular moment. The converse is also true and you are expected to observe other peoples' boundaries. If any members of the group are insensitive, talk to them. If they still do not accept your restrictions, talk to the leader. This is not an area to be bashful about. You have the right to ask that your values and limits be respected.

What are some of the things that can happen when a large group works together?

The group may respond as a unit with a strong focus, or it may subdivide into small and shifting groups. When there are subgroups, there may be an initial period of milling around sensing where to go, how and when to join an ongoing group. Some people may wait on the periphery, taking on the group's movement and soon becoming assimilated. The transition from one subgroup to another involves ascertaining what should be kept from the previous group and what needs to be left behind, as well as what new energy and focus will be explored next. People may entice one or two others to leave the ongoing group by presenting an attractive alternative, or they may burst in and scatter the group entirely. Of course, some subgroups may remain loyal, with each establishing a firm identity and only then interacting with other groups.

Do I always have to do what the group does?

In improv there is no "always." The group situation requires give and take; sometimes you'll go with the flow, sometimes you'll bide your time, sometimes you'll take the initiative. There is a time to cooperate and a time to take someone else's outlandish contribution even further; there is a time to break away on your own and counter with something completely new and different; and a time to lend support to the group encounter. A decision to change could begin subtly with a potential for growth; it could be outrageously startling yet so strongly motivated that it requires that you stick with it. After a while others may recognize, test, play with, or even oppose it. Or they may not respond at all. Maybe they did not see you or they saw but didn't find a connection between your material and their own. Rarely will it be because they are deliberately ignoring you.

Improvising in a group situation is not a testing of wills, but an exercise in teamwork. You want to feel good about your individual record, your contribution to the whole, and about the accomplishments of the group. Those are different but hardly mutually exclusive goals. As a matter of fact, it's quite wonderful when all are being generated and achieved simultaneously.

Sometimes I am sorta left flat.

Yes, that happens. In large group works where there are changing subgroups there may be a down time for an individual. That's all right. You have choices. You can join a group as soon as things are right again; or you can re-center and work alone, where your movements may invite others in.

In the group improv, I started a different movement but no one paid any attention. I was hoping that they would join in or react to what I was doing.

There are a couple of things at work here. Initially, have the courage to stay with a movement idea that counters the group. See how you can make it relate to what they are doing (relating can be complementary or contrary in nature). Possibly try weaving the new movement closely around them, perhaps touching them. Realize that they may be ready to acknowledge but not join you. Can you bridge the gap without forcing it? One way might be to go back to their movement and make a transition that entices them to follow, that maps the route. Or stamp it loudly, demanding them to notice and join in or meet your challenge in some fashion.

On the other hand, you should retain enough sensitivity so you know when to let go of your tangent and get back on board. Individuality for its own sake can be indulgent at best and alienating at worst.

Different people seem to bring out different movement qualities in me.

Yes, the same instructions with a different partner will create a different improv. Peers are agents of change; they trigger different responses.

We each had different images in that last improv. Really different!

Yes, at times you endow your partner with intentions that he is not specifically aware of. He may be simply playing with certain movement qualities, but he appears to you menacing and you respond accordingly. However, he is not neutral clay to be shaped by your perceptions; he is responding to his own agendas and fantasies as well as to you and your movements. This independence and privacy of our minds, combined with your openness to each other, allow both of you anonymity and the testing of a new self-knowledge. At the same time your partner's movement responses enable you to see your patterns in new ways, forcing a greater degree of objectivity. The friction of the encounter polishes self-definition.

What is the difference between taking the lead and dominating an improv?

In taking the lead there is a sense of responsibility; you are serving the intention of the improv. You will feel a satisfaction in what you are doing. As your courage grows and you are willing to take risks, new movements and directions happen. You generate energy and your ongoing drive allows automatic decisions which, by the nature of your concerns, are never at the expense of the group. Also you are loose with the reins; you allow the leadership to pass easily from you to someone else.

Dominance, on the other hand, is an ego trip. Your movements are not a result of group unity but of your personal agenda. You use everyone else for your own therapeutic ends or to make you look good.

If you care about the difference between the two, most likely you will know what that difference is and be interested in the first and on guard against the second.

What are the responsibilities of a mover during an improv?

Basically there are three—social, personal, and craft. The first can be reduced to common courtesy; courtesy is the oil that allows other things to happen. There is consideration for physical safety (controlling your physical outbursts enough so they do not endanger other people, spotting for someone if they find themselves in a precarious position), emotional safety (not criticizing people, making sure you are both a giver and a taker, a user and a provider), and social etiquette (arriving on time, and not using the session as a playground for your ego). Your social responsibility extends beyond the personal to a concern for the group as a whole. This includes realizing that the progress of each individual adds to the progress of the group and every member of the group, including you. Joining the class is agreeing to a social contract. You need to come to class, and you need to be on time—it is hard to join an improv that has started. You can't make up a class, for it will never happen again. You can't get notes, for the experience doesn't translate to paper. Inconsistent attendance not only impedes your own progress but it hampers the formation of strong group unity and identity.

Personal responsibility? Yes, of course. You're taking the course for a reason, or several reasons, ranging from wanting a creative workout, to needing a break from a tough mental schedule of physics, math, and chemistry classes, to wondering about the connection between people design and architectural design, to plain old curiosity and a love of things creative and/or physical. Honor your personal goals and be responsible to them; they're as valid as anyone else's.

Responsibility to the process and the craft is something else again, and not to be overlooked. Challenge yourself to go one step further (even if there is no one else in the room); stay with and trust the process (especially when the improv is not working so well); accept the instructions and do your best to realize them fully. Remember, improv serves you as you serve it; it is a symbiotic relationship.

If I don't feel good enough to dance, should I come to class?

It all depends. Sniffle? Yes. Sprained ankle? Yes. Depressed? Double yes! Virus? No. First of all, you can learn a lot by watching. Also, there are other active options: you can do a sit-down dance, accompany the improv on some percussion instruments, or be the external observer. "Handicapped" dances, resulting from a broken arm or blistered foot often force us to use parts of the body in unexpected ways. Providing accompaniment offers an opportunity to experiment with using a different medium to respond to the same motivation. Watching the improv lets you see objectively and to get involved in the discussion, furnishing a new perspective.

Here are some questions and discussions of interest to the more experienced improviser.

Lately it seems easier to get involved in an improv. It is almost as if I enter a different state of being.

Actually the first and most essential skill of improv is the ability to shift to the creative mode, to enter a state of *receptive readiness.* Mentally, it is a clear space—without preconceptions, hidden agendas, or carry-on baggage. You are totally present and secure in the here and now, neither tethered by the past, blinded by illusions, nor limited by expectations. You are centered, open, ready to meet and to be met, ready to jump into the void and accept the unexpected. It is an energized calm. A sense of eagerness prevails, tempered by a relaxed attention that combines patience with alertness. Such a solid yet energized base makes you dynamic enough to shift and accommodate, yet firm enough to keep focused and ignore irrelevant externals. The switch to readiness can become place specific, as when you walk in the door of the studio.

It sounds like a two-sided coin: a calm, almost unruffled serenity coupled with invigorated anticipation. Is that not contradictory?

It may seem so at first, but actually this dualism is exactly what's called for. There are other dualities as well. For instance, your attention is both global (seeing gestalts, perceiving relationships and forms not ordinarily paid attention to) and specific (noticing nuances). You become the fulcrum for visual, aural, kinetic, and tactile comprehension. All these intelligences transmit equally and are democratized as the verbal aristocracy crumbles. You adjust and listen impartially to inner and outer realities, giving each its due.

When you are properly centered, your initial perceivings and respondings are not filtered through verbal-logical censorships, but are overridden by curiosity, instinct, and a playful laissez-faire attitude. This mode accommodates the flash of insight, the "Aha!" of the creative process. The response is thus immediate and honest, unencumbered by questions and premature judgments; you are neutral, quintessentially fair and unbiased.

The idea of neutrality seems so blank.

Being neutral doesn't mean that you don't bring your true self to the improv or use your current condition and sensitivity for the work at hand. The difference is in orienting your psyche and attention to the instructions of the improv rather than to the problems you brought in the door. If those problems are relevant, they will surface easily enough, you may be sure. But the neutral point of origin will give you a calm place from which you can choose whether to escape the preoccupations of the day or confront them through the improv. Confrontation will occur on its own if and when the material brings you face to face with immediate concerns or deeper issues. For example, a woman once came to a session immediately after hearing of the death of a close friend. The leader was unaware of this. She was prepared not to move at all or to use movement only as a way to mourn her friend. Instead, quite contrary to her expectations, the improv became an affirmation and celebration of life.

We always talk about what it is like when an improv works. What is it like when it does not work?

It's no fun. There is no focus, intention, or passion. Work will be eclectic, superficial, hackneyed. Movement ideas will not develop or carry over from one person to another. Self-consciousness increases while genuine interaction decreases. People may stop moving, drop out, start talking.

But usually improvs do not go so completely or dramatically wrong. People might not realize the improv is a dud until after the fact; or it might not be working for only some of the people; or some individuals may think they are the only ones who can't get with it and instead of acting on that knowledge may pretend that things are fine, manufacture movement, and keep boringly busy.

Group work will lack a sense of the group. Awareness of oneself as a cog of the wheel will be missing, and in its place will be the singular wheel going its singular way in its own singular time frame.

Movement will neither partner nor mirror that of others; shapes will not puzzle-fit; timing, patterns, and rhythms will not be picked up, shared, and developed into ancillary variations. Ego identity will persevere. There will be neither anticipatory comprehension of others' response patterns nor a sense of expectations fulfilled and initiatives satisfied. There will be a failure to comprehend, identify, and respond to general as well as specific issues, including form (that is, to the overall dynamic shape of the piece and to the sensing of its conclusion).

When the group gets going there seem to be so many different things that happen.
   Yes, there is quite a variety in group work, yet there are some recurring patterns.
• Circles: facing in, out, holding hands, shoulder to shoulder, moving in, out, and around; a central figure (or figures) surrounded by others; standing, sitting, or on bellies, backs, or sides, radiating out like spokes of a wheel.
• A line (holding hands or not): snaking around the room, sometimes accelerating into snap-the-whip, then decelerating to a unified group movement or deteriorating to far-flung, smaller groups.
• Follow-the-leader: taking turns leading, often pausing for other types of interactions (for example, the leader starts to crawl and the second in line decides to climb aboard instead of also crawling; the third may then slide under, and so forth).
• Two or more groups, each working as a unit, with or without relating to each other.
• A unified group with solo or duet figures.
• Building body structures—as people wait to join they quietly watch in stillness, pace around assessing, or continue their previous involvement, keeping track through peripheral vision.
• Circlings or crossings: a solo figure circles around or cuts through everything else that is going on.

What about all the comings and goings within a group?
   Yes there can be great diversity and independence within a group improv.
• Individuals leave the group or subgroup and then return; they

interrupt, slide in gracefully or bring someone with them (ways in: exact repetition, mirroring, conversation, complementary, supplementary, or antagonistic movement).

• Individuals detach themselves from the group in anger or boredom, desiring or avoiding attention.

• An individual is active yet independent within the group.

• An individual goes to the sidelines.

• A duet or solo figure determines to change the movement or attitude of someone else. Sometimes they see themselves as benevolent ("she looked so all alone"). At other times they can be patronizing or even antagonistic, while taking a strange glee in their attempted control.

• A duet or solo figure considers it is their mission to gather all the rest of the groups together; sometimes they are extremely persistent. This often occurs near the end of an improv or session; they are determined that "we must all finish together."

Even though we never see each other outside of class, we are very close.

Sure. In the course of interacting with other people in improv, you become familiar not only with their movements but with their personalities and feelings. This is why a group which has worked intensively together, yet has no contact outside of the improv sessions, can have a closeness quite different from that shared by other friends. The mutual support and exposure of physical, creative, and emotional vulnerability creates a strong bond.

I can even work well with someone I don't like in movement improv.

In some cases you have to ignore the specific personality of the person you are moving with and simply start from neutral. At some level there is a detachment. "This is not Joe, whom outside of class, I don't really like, and even distrust a little; it is a responding body, and in this context we are really involved in the material, dancing up a storm, and using movement that demands mutual trust. It's wonderful." In a way, the detachment at one level allows you to be closer at another level. The improvisational environment provides a safety net; its isolation and atmosphere of trust creates a world unto itself.

What are the goals of an improv class?
• To explore, to experiment, to play, to form, to create.
• To get out of self and into self-in-movement, the deeper self that is often suppressed or unknown.
• To cull the courage to give up conscious decisions or control and trust intuitive choice-making.
• To find identity in movement; to try out different roles and explore a range of responses in order to achieve a larger and more flexible self-image.
• To become involved in a group process; to balance oneself between "a part of" and "apart from"; to yield to the group while maintaining one's basic responsibility as an individual.
• To become conscious of, and more skilled with, the expressive, communicative nature of movement.
• To have a good time.
• To get a physical workout.
• To get your fix for the day. (Fact: after ten minutes of intense physical movement, the brain secretes a natural tranquilizer.)

4 Creating a Conducive Environment

Improv, as an embodiment of the creative process, needs the proper environment in which to flourish, one that engenders trust, openness, readiness, drive, and passion. Creativity can't be forced to happen, but it can be encouraged and motivated.

THE LEADER

Creating a climate conducive to successful improvisation is heavily dependent on the skill, wisdom, and imagination of the leader. Yet the delicate, ever-changing, and unpredictable subtleties of improv make it impossible to say, "Do this and not that." There is a gray area where knowledge, spontaneity, personality, and process intertwine, calling for a unique response each time. Within this area the leader must achieve a dynamic, constantly shifting balance that avoids the erratic but includes the whimsical. Leading improvisation is neither simple nor automatic; like any skill, it takes time to learn and practice to master.

Of course it is not only the leader who influences the progress of the improv. Improv can be thought of as a traffic circle with the contributing elements being the leader, the improviser, and the ongoing improv itself. All three inform and affect one another, and it is their ongoing relationship that forms the gestalt.

Procedural Skills

The leader of an improv embodies a series of paradoxes: structured yet flexible, in control yet unobtrusive, sensitive yet not easily overwhelmed, patient yet time-conscious, idealistic yet realistic. Let us examine how each of these characteristics can best serve you as leader.

Structured Flexibility. First, of course, you must be organized.

49

You must know why you are using a given improv with a certain group at a particular time. It helps to know your immediate and long-range goals for the group so that you can choose an appropriate improv. Your choice should be based on an understanding of the part a particular improv plays in the greater developmental schema. Yet an improv is a living, growing entity; it emerges and undergoes mutations. In tending it you must continuously reassess and restructure. Be prepared for the improv to take off in new and surprising directions. Discern which directions have the potential to be fertile, nurture their growth, and be willing to abandon or alter your pre-set lesson plan in favor of the unexpected.

The ability to be this flexible includes, quite literally, the definitive aspects of the word *flexibility* itself: the ability to flex, to change, to bend with, and adjust to; to go, not at random, but as the need demands. For example, you are leading an improv and notice that some people are starting to work in pairs. You hadn't expected such a response; yet it has occurred organically, there are honest interactions taking place, and the people are still attending to the basic material of the improvisational structure you introduced. You respond by giving positive verbal recognition of the partnering, maybe even suggesting it as a possibility for others to explore.

You should also be flexible about altering your lesson plan for the session. You need to be open enough to trust the intuition that motivates your ideas, for such intuition has its own logic and validity. Perhaps, out of the blue, you get an idea for an improv; its possibilities excite you for "you know not what" reasons. You want to try it out, and the class level seems appropriate. By all means, go ahead and use it. Generally speaking, the more experience you have had in leading improvisation, the more likely it is that your undefined urge is worth pursuing.

Unobtrusive Guidance. In as open-ended a situation as improv, the built-in safety factor for the participants is knowing that there's a leader in control, that someone is giving form and guidance to an otherwise potentially chaotic situation. It helps when you are perceived as confident of your method, comfortable in your role, and willing to assume responsibility for the group. This is not the place for shyness or indecisiveness, yet your guidance should be tempered with wisdom and expressed unobtrusively.

Your style as a leader will jell with the experience of working with different groups and with a variety of improvs. As your style becomes familiar to your students, they become increasingly comfortable because they know they can count on a certain underlying consistency. You need not use your personality to jolt the student to heightened achievement. The range of the ideas and structures you provide should do that. Their responses to your material will provide enough excitement.

Realize that your own aesthetic preferences will influence the improv and the direction of the class. For instance, if you get bored with too many pedestrian solutions to problems you will probably automatically curtail those by giving directions which are difficult to carry out in a pedestrian mode. Yet if your style, preferences, and judgments are imposed too strongly, you will limit or even inhibit the movers. You should not be fulfilling your own creative needs but fostering those of the class. This necessitates that you provide a wide range of movement experiences, even if some of those are not your favorites. The guidance which you exercise and the limits and ranges which you set should advance the group, the improv, and the overall goals.

Sensitive Objectivity. Sensitivity is a must—to the needs of the group as a whole, to the needs of individuals within the group, to their attention span, and to their degree of readiness for change.

When difficult psychological situations crop up, the leader is home base. Your cool-headedness (not coldness) functions as ballast for the scary vulnerability that sometimes comes from the freedom to explore.

It is one thing to be sensitive (and make necessary adjustments as a result) and quite another to become so engulfed by empathy that you lose your ability to channel and direct the session. In such an instance you could easily become an insider, enmeshed in the improv, thus leaving the group essentially leaderless. A measure of professional detachment is needed to enable you to be sensitive enough to insure empathy and yet objective enough to guide the situation. Remember that the leader provides the outside eye to the inside feeling.

Patient Time-consciousness. Improvisation demands, first and foremost, lots of time. Don't rush from one instruction to the next, nor from improvisation to improvisation. Don't get antsy; it is not a race. Patience in the leader breeds a sense of ease in the improviser. But we do teach and dance in a time-conscious society, which imposes certain constraints. It is your responsibility to manage the class so that it concludes on time without rushing through the final moments.

There's another type of patience required as well. You must be prepared to wait through the long lengths of unimaginative movement that serves as breathing space between moments of divine inspiration. Often what is plain or commonplace to the external eye is significant to the doer, either in self-discovery or as groundwork for the future. Don't constantly look for nuggets of gold or assess results in terms of breakthroughs. They will happen in their own time.

Personal Traits

Must an improv leader be a dancer? Yes, of course, for the leader needs a rich personal source of improv, movement, and dance experiences to draw from. Dance improv is so kinesthetic that the major portion of what we know of it is by way of the sensorium; having that tacit knowledge makes us able to perceive, shape, and understand the experience. In addition, every leader needs certain personal characteristics: creativity, a sense of humor, and the ability to guide and elicit responses.

Creativity. Within the improvisational setting, you as the leader must be quick-witted and resourceful, able to take off on new tangents while at the same time linking them to the structure at hand in imaginative ways. In a sense you must be a poet, ever ready to generate powerful images, metaphors, and analogies, for your input is largely verbal, and what works as an image for one individual or group won't always work for another. Creativity is called for not only in the act of leading but in developing ideas that will add verve, excitement, and insight to the experience. While as an improv leader you need to be creative, you should have creative outlets other than your improv class, so that the class does not become the only forum for your creative energy. It is not a place for you to impress others with your talents, but a special opportunity to help others to find and develop their own creative potential and their delight with motion.

Sense of Humor. While a sense of humor is a desired trait for any teacher, it is essential for a leader of improv. Anyone who takes himself, life, or dance too seriously keeps others at a distance and encourages them to do the same. A sense of humor goes hand-in-hand with a sense of play and an easy attitude. Things should become neither overly heavy nor precious.

This easy attitude will also allow you to recognize and encourage funny things that happen in the improv situation. You do not need to artificially create humorous situations nor be a stand-up comic in order to enjoy or elicit humor. Oddity, silliness, and fun happen spontaneously; all they need is the permission to be developed. Sometimes humor will come from a sense of surprise or of being uncomfortable with some of the unusual confrontations or combinations that happen. These funny sparks can serve as tension breakers. The wise leader capitalizes on humor and flights of whimsy to add spice to the improv situation. Be easy with and enjoy such moments for their own sake. You may want to try **Stomach Laugh** as an exercise in fun. Or you may actually want to try some improvs geared toward the comic. (See the unit on Art Forms in chapter 14, "Sources.") Realize that a sense of playfulness can produce good work. So take it seriously when need be, or tongue-in-cheek when that's appropriate.

One Who Can Draw Forth. In order to make an improvisation happen, the leader must be someone who can evoke the elusive process of creativity and coax it into existence in others. Nowhere are the words of John Martin truer than in this realm: "A teacher can't put in; she must draw forth." That is the real challenge of an improv leader—drawing forth.

Quite naturally, you'll become very involved in the creative progress of the mover. You nurture his sense of self and join him on his journey, providing sanctuary while challenging him to extend himself and fulfill his potential. It is because the atmosphere is safe, nonjudgmental, and caring that you *can* challenge, sometimes gently, sometimes subtly, but also at times directly. The intent of such challenges is to propel the individual into a direction and manner that is his own, but not yet realized. You perceive the latent energy and beauty, and your expectation for seeing it realized is often what gives the mover the courage to go one step farther. You must be a vision-prompter, a catalyst, a shaman.

THE ATMOSPHERE

The crucial element here is trust. If the movers trust themselves and the situation they are in, they will be willing to open up, to put themselves on the line. When they feel free to respond honestly, the door is open to creative movement. Your job is to insure that the conditions conducive to such a response are present. It is for you to generate an atmosphere where explorations, experiments, and risks can take place safely. You must see that each person is accepted, respected, and dealt with equally; that no one is judged or compared; and that each mover is helped to shape his experience so as to make it meaningful for him.

The improvisers must feel confident of your tolerance and receptivity. They cannot try out new things if they're concerned with how they look, if they're worried about the right-or-wrongness of something they may do, or if they're afraid of being put down, made fun of, or singled out. The improvisational act must be a fairly anonymous one for the mover; we can do all sorts of things in private that we would not be likely to do in the public spotlight. It becomes your responsibility to allow each improviser the freedom of anonymity, thereby fostering the taking of a chance, the attempting of something unusual or different for that individual.

Because experience has shown that no two groups or individuals ever react in the same way to any given problem or structure, it is particularly important for the mover to know that there are no expected "solutions." Expectations are boxes, sealed rooms; in improv we want to create hallways, open doors, gazebos, and Grand Central Stations. The leader does not look for set stimulus-response patterns but for variegated attempts and discoveries. Of course, things don't always work out; that's the chance one takes when working with the unpredictable.

When the discussion makes it evident that an improv was awful, or useless, or boring, investigate the cause. Was it the fault of timing, location, material, presentation, or appropriateness? Seeing the leader eagerly trying to identify the problem and accepting responsibility for it is yet another way of promoting trust. Your honesty encourages their own, a feeling of mutual concern is engendered, and human trial-and-error is given a positive rather than a negative vote, thus making risk-taking more acceptable.

The atmosphere you create needs to say, "Discover, create, find your own answers, and relationships. Help make the puzzle; don't solve it before you yourself explore it." Then the mover will realize that what he does is okay, be it simple, brilliant, awkward, unique, or mundane. He will be able to trust his responses and feel free to talk about them afterward. His trust comes from the atmosphere created by a leader who encourages his experiments by using positive reinforcement and who provides a dance experience that is enjoyable, invigorating, and capable of being insightful.

Citings of specific moments ("It was stunning when Adam and Stacey did a lunge or drop-roll at the same moment across the room from each other; were the two of you aware of it happening?") affirms the leader's concentration on their work. It makes the movers appreciate the leader's perception of the situation as a whole and raises their consciousness about the exciting things that improvisation engenders.

Trust in peers is also important and needs to be developed gradually, carefully. Initial exercises that promote physical trust are **Back-to-Back, Trust Circle, Create-a-Trust,** and others. (See the unit on Trust and Relaxation in chapter 14, "Sources.") These in turn generate emotional trust, especially when they are supported and reified with discussions about the feelings and images invoked, as well as the misconceptions or concerns which arose. Having fun, sharing responsibility, and working with different individuals are necessary factors in group improv. Developing trust and working as a group are important because improvisation carries with it a responsibility for the members of the group to care about each other—not necessarily as friends, but as mutual improvisers who are all struggling with their own creative impulses, blocks, ruts, fears, cautions. An attitude of acceptance of each other's work and worth therefore becomes paramount. It will evoke a willingness to honor the sanctity and privacy of what occurs within the improvisational setting. The extent to which one person is trusted by others will be the extent to which he is able and willing to be open, honest, and truly explorative himself.

As the group identity grows, so will the positive feelings about the group's unity and importance. The strength that comes from belonging to such a group will in turn feed each individual; it will grow as the group continues to work as a collective unit, sharing and commiserating, enjoying and discovering. Each group will quite unwittingly create its own tenor and characters. As its personality emerges, the leader's way of dealing with that group becomes accordingly more specifically tailored to it.

The leader says in every way possible (verbally and nonverbally): "You are safe here; we value you, your ideas, and your participation; we honor your right as a member of this group to make some of the decisions. We accept you, as sometimes more aggressive, as an initiator or leader, sometimes more passive or receptive, as a follower or an observer. Your enthusiastic participation and your cautious hesitation each have a valid part to play. We expect you to push yourself beyond your own comfortable limits, believing it a requirement for growth and expansion; but we will also respect your setting limits on how far is too far. In saying this, we assume and expect you to take responsibility for identifying when those limits are reached. You are our richest resource, and we value your input."

5 Leaders' Concerns

Am I responsible for warm-ups?

Yes, if an improv session has not been preceded by physical exercise for all members of the group, you must take it upon yourself to provide a warm-up. Some good ideas include: improvised non-repetitive stretching (which allows for accommodation to needs of the moment), a repetitive ritual movement sequence (which you or they specifically design), or an initial improv structure (perhaps as the introduction to your first improv). Another possibility is pedestrian movement; simple walking, swaying, and running are all ways of breaking inertia and putting the body in motion. The body's relation to gravity and energy is called into play as coordination of parts spontaneously occurs. Since movers tend to start improvising gradually, easing into images and movements before charging full-speed ahead, the warm-up need not be elaborate or extensive. A good idea in planning the class is to begin with the gentler improvs and proceed on to the more energetic ones.

However, if you are working with trained dancers, you will have to take extra care. Like race horses, they need thorough attention in this area. If at all possible, have their improv session follow a technique class. In lieu of that you could create an improv sequence based on basic vocabulary that includes pliés; twists and rotations; foot articulations; back, neck, and leg stretches; swings and extensions.

How about getting them psychologically prepared to improvise. It is really different from a physical warm-up.

That's true. There are a number of different ways to achieve receptive readiness. (See discussion at the end of chapter 3, "Beginners's Questions.") We'll describe a few, but you can certainly create your own. Basically they fall into three categories: visualization, midbrain movement (involving the cerebellum), and repetitive or ritualistic activity.

Visualization

Start standing or lying down. Visualize all your tensions dissolving and draining from the top of your head down into the earth. Now connect with gravity, establishing a rootedness. Draw energy from a universal, inexhaustible source. Let that energy radiate up through your body, connecting with the breath. Let your breathing get deeper and affect your entire body.

Mid-Brain Warm-up

Start standing or lying down. Imagine a small puddle of oil in the palm of each hand. Move your hands around so the oil can get deep into the joints, muscles, knuckles, fingertips. Let the flow be easy, continuous, sinuous, no sudden starts or stops. Let the oiling proceed up through the wrist, lower arm, and elbow. Then onto the shoulders with smooth continuous movement. *Once one part of the body gets oiled, it continues to move in the same way;* it does not stop. Continue to oil the rest of your body with the sinuous motion. Once every part is in motion, keep the sustained flow and move a little faster, then faster still. Don't get jerky; keep the sense of ongoingness, no jolts or punctuations, just an overall, never-ending motion.

Ritual

Starting each session with a set movement pattern or ritual is a unifying tactic that also serves as a psychological grounding. Created rituals work if they are well designed, taken seriously, incorporate basic elements of rhythm and repetition, and demand strict adherence. Reference to a symbol or a natural phenomenon can make it more powerful.

All these approaches give the mover a neutral but kinesthetic focus; they provide a way to start sensing the body and heighten awareness of bodily systems and parts. They orient us away from the events of the day and toward the concentrated presence that improv requires.

You may always start with the same warm-up, or you may vary it according to the day or specific improv you are leading off with. Or, after experimenting with several, you might allow the individual mover to reach her receptive readiness according to the mode she prefers.

Any of these techniques can also be used as a cooling down at the end of a session by gradually lowering the speed and/or energy and opening perception to the world beyond improv.

I was asked to teach improv but the only space available was a huge gym.

It's okay. While a clean, warm dance studio is ideal, you can work in lots of places. A huge space can be inhibiting, so you must take steps to create a more intimate and protective atmosphere. Reduce the space by marking off a smaller working area (using screens, chairs, or even a row of shoes and dance bags). Insure development of territoriality by always using the same part of the space, delineated in the same way. Select improvs for each session that include circle forms or other spatial and psychological orientations that will deepen the sense of community. Be happy you don't have a place that's too small (of course, a solution for that is to divide the group and have half watch and half do).

Basically, what is important is that the space be clean, free of clutter, quiet and private and that the working site is (or is made to be) relative to the size of the group.

What about the size of the group?

Obviously this is sometimes contingent on the size of the space. The group should be large enough to get lost in, but not so big that it diminishes possibilities for taking the lead. An ideal working size is between eight and twenty, but improv can be a glory for one and a celebration with two hundred so long as the leader takes the number of participants into account in designing the improv and dealing with the results.

What about when you have an odd number of participants but the structure calls for paired work?

Have someone sit out and observe, being sure to rotate this status. It is not a good idea to accommodate this person by being his partner; it is impossible to do him justice as an involved improv partner and still be responsible for leading. Sitting out is fine; they learn a lot.

They want me to teach at 8 A.M.! That can't be right!

Don't worry: if they can get there, you can get them going. Actually almost any time is fine; an early session finds people fresh, and a late one can be wonderful for releasing the built-up tensions of the day or clearing the mind and letting go. After lunch is slow; the inertia of full stomachs is difficult to overcome. Occasionally scheduling a sunrise, sunset, or midnight session capitalizes on additional elements as new resources—and can often be a shot-in-the-arm toward unity and sanctity.

How long should a class be?

The length of class varies with the purpose, but a class devoted only to improv should be between forty minutes and two hours. Too short doesn't allow for successful building of momentum, exploration, and completion through discussion. For beginners, a one-hour class twice a week is probably better than a two-hour class once a week. Too long can be physically draining or emotionally overpowering, although some particular goals may call for marathon sessions (as in a retreat or at an intensive workshop, when the aim is to break down barriers and forcefully push people to go beyond their limits into new territory).

How much material should I bring to each session?

Lots. Some groups (especially children) eat up material. Better to have too much than not enough. You can always use the leftovers another time.

Can the improvs in this book be used exactly as given?

They are offered as ideas, examples, and guides. The ones in "Sources" (chapter 14) are presented in skeletal form. Some in the text are spelled out, to give you an idea of the kinds of elaboration available. Of course you won't read them verbatim. Perhaps you'll just use the beginning or the image, developing it in your own way. During your initial leading experiences, you might feel comfortable having some notes to refer to, but after you have given an improv several times, that won't be necessary. You need to know the improv's theme, the types of options that you want to cultivate, and the various inducements to creative exploration. Other than this, be open and allow your stream of consciousness to respond to the movers' actions. Cultivate thinking on your feet. As you and the group gain experience in translating images into movement, you can play the poet, adding more metaphors and abstract images.

Sometimes I can't get my instructions succinct enough. There's so much I want to say. I get so wordy! Help!

Welcome to the club. Relax. It takes experience to be elegantly succinct. If you identify this as a problem, spend a bit more time planning, maybe even sketching out key words or phrases to home in on. You can always use the discussion to bring up the things you had trouble saying or left out for the sake of brevity. You'll find similar situations repeating themselves and soon you and your group will develop an understanding. The one crucial thing is to make the group understand that they should continue to move while you talk; then you'll have plenty of time to say what you need. But don't panic—the space you leave between your instructions is where the work gets done.

How structured or detailed should an improv for beginners be?

Defining limits actually is a way to open doors. By providing a focus, and parameters within which to explore the instructions, you offer security: a place to start, a direction to go, and a time to conclude. For an inexperienced group, start with a limited number of choices and gradually add more choices. Here is an improv you could try.

Walk in Straight Lines
Walk simply in straight lines. Vary the speed. Settle on one tempo and play with the rhythm of your walk. Add to the rhythm with various parts of your body, clapping, stamping, and snapping. Include going to the floor but come back up again and continue with the walk. Keep the lines straight. Occasionally add moments of silence and stillness. Interrupt the rhythmic straight lines or the moments of stillness with continuous or sustained movements that shape or sculpture the space around you.

At first, this improv is quite limited (walk in straight lines). The options then introduced are also limited within themselves (vary speed). Soon the possible responses to the overall accumulation of options becomes quite complex, but because they were considered one by one, they are not overwhelming. By the end of the improv the movers have been guided toward making many choices. This teaches them the skill of building complexities and manifold responses. The progressions and possibilities you spell out soon become internalized, and in ensuing improvs they will need fewer directions from you. In this way they will also learn basic ways of dealing with movement. For instance, by adding counterpoint (silence or sustained molding in the above improv) they learn that opposites can work together to highlight the primary material.

Sometimes beginners seem intimidated by very emotional and dramatic images.

In the earliest stages of working with beginners it is best to stay away from such images. Many beginners are self-conscious enough about responding freely and simply in movement without being asked to bare their inner souls. Conversely some beginners *do* hunger to get right into the depth of it all; acknowledge their experiences but have your instructions and lesson plans start with simple movement suggestions, for the rest of the group may not be so eager to dive in. In either case, familiarity with movement will soon lead to greater self-expression and self-revelation.

After they have worked awhile, what about asking them to dance "how they feel"? What's wrong with that?

Theoretically, nothing. But to ask someone to "dance how you feel" is a tall order for someone who first, has never tried to transform emotions into movement (much less dance) and second, doesn't really know how he feels at that particular moment. It provides no starting place, no handles to grab hold of. By contrast, consider an improv that builds pathways between sensory feeling and emotional feeling.

The Wall

Imagine that there is a wall surrounding you. Explore its surface. What is it made of—glass? Gauze? Sound? Stone? Feel it with your back, hip, or other body parts. Is it firm? Yielding? Alive?

What is its temperature? Color? Is having the wall there secure and comforting? Show that calmness. Is it restrictive? Does it make you angry? Want to break out? Try to press against it, gently or with force, quickly or in a sustained manner. Is it resistant or flexible? Exaggerate that. Be sensitive to how you feel about the size, shape, and resiliency of the wall, its height and thickness. Does it remind you of some space you have been in before? Respond accordingly.

This improv allows for a range of "how it feels" responses, from hateful to tender. An open-ended but well-defined structure was provided; movement and movement-oriented words were injected throughout. Within that structure, the mover is free to interpret the wall image according to his impulse at that moment. He has the opportunity to identify exactly how he does "feel."

Another point this improv makes is that improvisation is not always pretty. It runs the gamut of human experience. Indeed, one of its exciting aspects is that it provides a forum for exploring a full range of human emotions.

I understand that you have to use movement words with beginners, but how basic do you have to be?

The words used for instructions have to evoke a movement response, not just a movement image. For instance, a bubbling brook is a beautiful movement image, but a beginner may not immediately perceive how to translate it into bodily movement. An advanced student will not have any trouble: she will know how to abstract the movement from the image and transform it to a physical state. Of course, there are many possibilities. She may travel its winding path, employing its erratic accumulation of speed and its twisting accommodation of the stones. Or she may begin with a bubbly feeling slowly simmering inside that builds from her belly; plays along her torso, enveloping arms, neck, fingers; and gradually washes over her whole body resulting in undulations or little energy bursts. Many beginners will need help in making this transference.

In the initial work with beginners should you start with improvs that do not call for much depth of involvement?

Different leaders will have different responses to this question: "Yes, break the ice first." "No, the first order of business is to addict them to in-depth responses."

What about self-consciousness, especially with people new to improv or dance?

Any new environment or activity breeds a certain amount of tension, wariness, and insecurity. And so the beginner, regardless of the strength of his self-image or his pride as a dancer or athlete (that is, as a master of movement), may feel certain inhibitions. Self-consciousness has far more to do with psychology than with past training or expertise. There is no fixed correlation between technical skill and the tendency to feel self-conscious in the improvisational setting. Arlie was a beautifully trained dancer with a lot of performing experience who, when she first tried improv, was severely inhibited and stilted in her responses. She used only technical vocabulary and was constantly concerned with how she looked, with the "correctness" of her movements. She said repeatedly, "I'm just not creative. I can't do this stuff." Curiously enough, this was in the same class as a six-foot-two, 210-pound man who had never taken a dance class in his life, but who would try all sorts of things in movement without any concern for its outward appearance. Because he did not worry about *dancing* or being creative, all kinds of movement and interactions happened. Repeated participation is the best antidote; familiarity reduces tensions and builds security, thus allowing the individual fuller participation with greater ease.

How can the leader help?

Self-consciousness comes from embarrassment, of feeling on-the-spot, or uncomfortably noticed, and it is harmful because it is restrictive, obscuring even the perceptive awareness of how something feels. Basically, when people are very involved in moving they forget to be self-conscious. Try directing the focus away from the self and toward the experience. For example, attention could be directed to the shadows made by the moving bodies rather than the makers thereof, or to the points of ground contact, or to the necessity of speed in executing a set of directions. Such redirection leads to heightened absorption in the movement and helps bypass or subvert self-consciousness.

I have seen people so nervous that they can't stop giggling.
Yes, these self-conscious crazies may come when a person feels threatened by a close, confrontational situation or by the pressure to be too emotional or too physical. Uncontrolled giggling is very disruptive, not to say contagious. If toned-down instructions do not help, have her sit out and watch or even leave the room until she can be calm and focused.

Isn't there a good kind of self-consciousness?
Yes. There is a heightened sense of self, an awareness of the self in action, a refined consciousness of perceptions and responses, a non-judgmental observer. This takes time to develop. It is one of the skills of improvising.

What function does a leader's commentary play during the improv itself?
During the period of the improv, occasional comments such as "nice," "good work," "ahh, lovely," "yes, yes; keep going" let the movers know they are working well. You encourage them to continue with a moment and movement that they may or may not have realized was worthwhile. You reinforce a process which inexperienced improvisers may be feeling skeptical about and assure them that you are paying attention and serving as an observant eye.

What is the best way of observing what's going on without seeming like an intruder?
Let your gaze drift over the whole group, so no one person feels singled out. Keep a comfortable distance. Recently a leader-in-training kept coming within a foot or two of the people in her group, watching them carefully and commenting quite positively on their responses. Even though her verbal feedback was supportive and encouraging, it caused a self-consciousness which precluded deeper involvement. It is difficult for even confident

improvers to keep a deep level of involvement when someone is breathing down their back.

Should I participate in the improv?

Tempting though that may be, it is best that you do not. Maintain your separate identity from the group. The desire to move with them is often self-indulgent—you want to set an example, to show off, to have as much fun as they are having. Inevitably, your participation limits your ability to watch, assess, and take action.

An exception might be if you are observing a student-leader. Observing from the sidelines will give you one measurement of his effectiveness, but participating in the improv will give you quite a different one.

If you have an advanced group that has been together for a long time you may occasionally pass the role of leader around, giving yourself and others a chance to interact at a different level.

What if they just aren't getting it? Can I demonstrate then?

Not with beginners; as soon as you move they take that movement as *the way*. That assumption immediately limits them, no matter what you say. If you have to demonstrate because you can't get the concept across verbally, do something simple and direct. Physically define your verbal terms but don't dance for them. Otherwise all they see is how beautifully, skillfully, or creatively you move, and may quickly conclude that's how it's supposed to be, or that they can't do as well. The result is that they might miss the point of your demonstration and become concerned about their inadequacy. There is one alternative to showing something with simplicity, and that is by doing it so outrageously that they wouldn't dream of copying you. (Simple-minded or tongue-in-cheek demonstrations do have their place.)

What other options do I have?

You can use your voice. If you're trying to elicit a strong movement with power and commitment, do a simple punch and let out a room-splitting scream. This usually startles them into thinking, "If she can do that, I can at least . . . " Although they may have fully understood that you were asking for a display of strength, the usual social "statute of limitations" was probably at work, causing them to temper their responses into more "acceptable" degrees of display. Your pushing those unstated but well-known limits automatically opens the door that much further for them to do the same.

Remember that your voice is the link between you and the movers. Aside from jolting them into action, try varying the way you speak so as to make it congruent with what you want to elicit—light and quick when inviting movement of that sort, slow or deep when instigating ponderous force. Your voice, as an instrument, should support the physical mood you want to evoke.

Somehow my timing seems off when I lead. Is there a way to fix that?

Timing is essential for an improv leader, just as it is for every great performer and politician. Much mediocrity has been saluted as brilliant, and much wisdom has fallen by the wayside, simply because of timing—in the first instance superb, in the second, abysmal. Timing in leading an improv is best improved by experience. When leading, allow yourself a certain degree of vicarious participation; try to have part of you "in" the group as they move. Sensitive observation often lets you give the next cue as if it was the perfect time to do so. Nevertheless realize that each person's timing is different, so you will always be a little soon for some and a bit late for others. But it will be fine for most; people are amazingly adaptive. It helps to realize that you walk the thin line between the paired concerns of keeping the pace going and providing time for involvement and exploration. It takes time for an idea to find its way into the muscles and neurons, time for it to become a part of the hands and hips, the head and heart.

One of the best ways to check your timing is by evaluating the improv. Did it go somewhere? Did you notice any annoyance at, or resistance to the insertion of new instructions? Were they ready to bring the improv to a conclusion before you were? Keep track, and see if the answers to any of these questions indicate recurring problems. Another way to check is through the discussion, perhaps specifically asking for comments. The best advice, especially for a beginning leader, is to take two more very slow breaths before assuming a change is needed. But basically let your restlessness be your guide.

Sometimes I find myself moving around on the side while I try to figure out how to say the next part of the instructions.

Yes, that happens. The leader sometimes has to move to get the experiential knowledge she needs in order to transform her kinetic knowing into verbal instructions.

Sometimes I get mixed up on the use of the terms: abstract, literal, and objective, subjective. Can you help?

Yes, while each term seems clear, they are sometimes hazily or confusingly applied. Let's first review the fact that movement can be *abstract, literal,* or *abstracted* (see the discussion of abstraction in chapter 2, "Experiential Body of Knowledge"). Here is an illustration.

An *abstract* movement:	a phrase of pure movement for arm and hand, having no external reference.
A *literal* movement:	a hand-and-arm gesture of blowing a kiss.
An *abstracted* movement from the above gesture:	the arm circles the head, stops in front of the face, then extends forward; the fingers wriggle and fan out.

Subjective and *objective* refer to one's perception of the movement, either as a mover-creator or observer. Here are two different perceptions (one subjective and one objective) of the abstracted movement given above.

subjective:	as I perform (or view) this, I feel a sense of tenderness wash over me; this is a poignant moment.
objective:	as I perform (or view) this, I notice the intricacies of the timing, the need for specific coordination, and the fluid results; I admire the clever construction of the movement and the phrase.

The objective-subjective perception is independent of the literal-abstract issue. The fact that we can have disparity in perceptions makes it possible for a great deal of variety in responses and makes discussions of improvs and dance concerts controversial, fun, frustrating, and ultimately enlightening.

It seems that this would also apply to the instructions. Wouldn't it be possible to give the same instructions two different ways?
Sure. Let's try.

An Abstract or Pure Movement Approach: Getting Out I
Take a curled up, very contained position. Using fast, intense, high energy, move out of that position to a large standing position. You may move any part of your body only one inch at a time. But you must move very quickly.

A Literal or Dramatic Approach: Getting Out II
You are in a small restrictive place where you have been for a long time. The space is getting smaller, making you extremely uncomfortable. You have to escape, but it is difficult and you can only get one part of your body out at a time, inch by inch. You are nervous that your escape will be blocked.

I wonder how different they would look?
Try an experiment. Divide the group into three sections. Give the first section the dramatic instructions and the second the pure movement instructions. Section three doesn't know what the instructions were. Its job is to watch each group (one at a time) and report what images (if any) were evoked and how the two sections differed (if indeed they did).

What improvs would you recommend for early group experiences?
Try **Rhythm Circle.** While it is a good group improv for any level, it provides a strong unifying experience for beginners. Precede it with a couple of the basic relating improvs such as **Back-to-Back, Mirroring,** or **Conversation.**

Rhythm Circle
Run around the room seven times, gradually getting faster, keeping your weight low; then find a place lying on your back and listen to all the sounds inside and outside your body. Go. Listen.

Let the different pulses settle into one rhythm, and put that in one part of your body. Let me see that reflected rhythm. It can be very small, just a finger, a foot, your head. Put it in a different part of your body, another. Have two parts moving to that same rhythm or let it travel from one part to another. Get your entire body involved with the rhythm. Don't let it stop; it should be continuous; you will work with it for a long time. Gradually *let the movement take you* to sitting. Don't just sit up; but allow the pulsing to bring you up. Then let the movement take you to kneeling, crawling. Finally it brings you to your feet. As it overcomes your entire body, begin traveling. Keep connected to your rhythm; let me see it in your body and hear it in your feet. Keep your own rhythm strong and don't let the others confuse or change it. Start to travel around the room counterclockwise. Now open your awareness to all the various rhythms and sounds which are going on. As a group, begin to find a common rhythm. Be willing to give up yours to join the group. [Give them time, but if they have trouble, help them by clapping a rhythm.] Stay with the new rhythm; make it strong. [If you are using a drummer he should come in at this point, picking up the group's rhythm.] Become aware of the entire circle. You are part of a community, the community of the circle. In the center of the circle there is something sacred which the group must always protect from evil. In your mind's eye see what that is. Each of you contributes to the group's identity and strength and to the sacredness of the object within the circle. When you are ready, cross the center of the circle doing movement that is very different in rhythm or quality from the movement you are doing now on the outside of the circle. You can go very slow, fast, crawl, roll, leap. There can be up to five people crossing at one time [depending on the size of the group—up to one-third]. As you cross, relate to the sacred object. Cross at least three times; go when you are ready. . . . Cross again, this time spending more time in the center. Notice what others in the center are doing and see if you can pick up some of their movement and relate to them. Stay awhile and work with them. This time there can be more people in the center at one time. Go when you are ready. Go at least three times. . . . Let the activity in the center grow; stay there as long as you like; there can be as many people as you want in the center. As a group, decide where it should go from here.

What kind of responses have you had with this improv?

They have varied considerably. Sometimes the movement around the circle is compelling, elaborate, and very individualistic. Other times it is a simple walk or run with all the more creative responses happening in the center. Often the center activity consists of solos or small groups, with the movers faithfully returning to the outside of the circle to participate in the ongoing group rhythm protecting the center. At other times there is a rush of many people to the center with only a lone mover maintaining the circle and keeping vigil. Often the circle is lost for a while but returned to at the end.

Rhythm Circle was given to three different groups on the same day, and their responses varied greatly. All were high school juniors. None had tried improv before; for all it was their fifth session together and their first improv as a group. The day was extremely hot (95°) and humid; they were all sure they could not move, much less dance. The improvs lasted about thirty minutes. While the movement responses were not radically different in groups A and B, their perception of what happened was.

Group A became completely involved in the images of tribal happenings and good and evil. They wanted to discuss the improv extensively, even the next day. At one point the circle was too small and they were asked to make it larger; there was a great reluctance. Afterward one student asked "Why did you want to kill us?" She explained, "You told us that evil was outside the circle, then you told us to make the circle larger! Why did you want us to die?"

Group B ran and clapped various rhythms the entire time and spent only perfunctory time crossing the center. "The rhythm really carried me." When asked about images, none had any and they had no desire to discuss the improv at all.

Group C was very inventive with group movement. They moved in and out of many formations, some reminiscent of children's games. Unlike A and B, they dissolved the circle altogether to serve the need of the day, forming a line that snaked around, left the room, got a drink of water, and returned to form a new line formation, waiting for the others before continuing as a group. At one point they added bebop vocals, and at another, people broke out one at a time and performed a jazzy solo. This group was delighted with the various material that emerged from the improv and enjoyed identifying the many references, but otherwise had no real desire for extended discussion.

Since the responses can be so different, would it be okay to give it (or other improvs) more than once to the same group?
Sure. Improvs can be repeated. No improv is ever the same twice. In the **Rhythm Circle,** after the initial time you can truncate the preparation: "Run, stand, rhythm in different parts of the body, travel into circle...." You can completely skip the images of the sacred circle. Or you can try a variation that starts with a different kind of energy, for example, "While standing, turn fast and slow until you are dizzy; move the dizziness; find a rhythm, let me hear it in your feet as you move, travel around the room in a circle...."

*Why does the **Rhythm Circle** work so well?*
It works well because it incorporates fundamentals of our human physiology and psychology and molds them into a social framework. The heartbeat (exaggerated by the initial running around the room) is the most natural and familiar rhythm, supporting and underlying all we do. The circle is a traditional community-building formation, often engendering feelings of protection. It easily translates to good versus evil, or to a sense of worship, giving it religious or supernatural overtones. From a focused, very specific, yet simple and individualized beginning, the improv progresses naturally toward a driving, unified group experience.

*Could I give this as a sample introductory improv without any preparation, such as **Mirroring** or **Conversation?***
Actually it does work as a one-shot initiation to improv. The tribal experience always amazes beginners. People sometimes feel a little strange at first, but then find "it's fun." With first-timers the amount of relating that goes on in the center of the circle is minimal; that's why we suggest preceding it with some partnering improv. When presenting this as an isolated experience it would help to have a drummer to add support, definition, and drive.

Does it always work?

No. The **Rhythm Circle,** like any other improv, sometimes just does not work well, even with the suggested preparation. Occasionally a group resents the entire beginning but gets involved in the circle; another will respond only when let free with "As a group decide where it should go from here." So far we have not found a foolproof improv.

What about the ending of an improv?

The important thing is to be clear about the difference between ending and just stopping. When it is appropriate, give some advance notice: "Finish what you are doing. Let it take as long as it needs to, and then end. There is no rush."

With beginners you may want to assist by talking them through a conclusion. Stop giving them choices in the instructions. Reduce the number of possibilities: "Find one place in the room to be." Lower the energy level or the speed: "Let the movement become slower, softer." Narrow the focus: "Zero in on one aspect and let other concerns slip away." These reductions help create a physical or dramatic necessity to bring the piece to an end.

When you don't want to dictate the nature of the conclusion, simply indicate that people now have the freedom to "let the movement find its own ending." This implies that there is more to an ending than just stopping and that there is something else at work, a form that needs resolution, a motivation that has to be clarified and worked out. With this approach you give them the responsibility of making sure their curiosity has been satisfied, the contingencies explored, the interesting material developed, and the relations resolved. Encourage the movers to use the natural phenomena of phrasing and momentum to bring closure.

At the conclusion of a group improv you may want to wait one more breath before you acknowledge the end, because sometimes they'll start up again. This is a delicate moment, however, because sometimes the revival is triggered by uncertainty rather than by organic necessity. Sometimes there is a valid need for a coda or recapitulation, or a strong urge for a whole new beginning. You and they must learn to listen carefully for these.

Does an improv ever end with a high burst of energy?

It can. The usual tendency is for an ending to be somewhat subdued and contained. This is especially true with large groups which, as a unit, bring the energy down and the rhythm to a conclusion. Often they curl tightly around each other or disperse to their own corners. The movers slow down because they need to read each other and sense that they all agree that it really is the end. It is hard for twenty people to decide simultaneously to suddenly stop. Of course the group could be guided: "Gradually keep this movement building in intensity, get faster, pull it in ... tighter, faster, so tight and fast that you will have to explode! End with that burst."

If a high energy ending were agreed upon in advance ("at the highest energy point all rush headlong to the sides of the room," a group that has been working together for a long time might find that moment independently of a leader's guidance.

For more ideas of ending at a high point see chapter 8, "Create Your Own Improv."

How long does an improv usually take?

An improv can be a two-to-five-minute shorty, done to illustrate a point in composition class; it could be a ten-second, across-the-floor sequence in technique class, in which individuals choose the order and number of leaps, falls, and rolls that they want. Long improvs, on the other hand, can last somewhere between five minutes and an hour or more. The point is that each improv has its own length, determined by the goal, the group's responses, and an inherently appropriate form.

What is the function of the discussion?

The discussion after an improv is a complementary part of the process. It is an opportunity to identify concerns and communicate about what happened. Talking gives verbal formulation to an otherwise amorphous, intuitive experience while its reflective nature adds objectivity and critical awareness. Feedback from the leader and/or observers adds a wider perspective to each person's own sense of the experience. People hear how others saw a certain action, or how a co-mover interpreted it. Contradictory remarks often function as eye-openers rather than being confrontational.

Discussion provides answers (or at least speculations) on such things as: "What was everyone doing when I was in the middle on my belly with my face down?" "How did you feel when we struck out at you?" "How did we all know to go to the floor at the same time?"

Things identified in the discussion are likely to be noticed when they happen again in another framework. Soon they are savored, extended, sharpened, polished. Larger patterns, realizations, and associations grow; improvs become richer and more finely articulated. The group's awareness of itself and of its members becomes more familiar and thus more intimate, allowing, and complex.

Discussion also provides a time to clarify procedures, assumptions, and expectations. "But I was sure we had to _____." The sooner misconceptions are cleared up, the better.

How do I lead the discussion? How can I get it started?
The leader sets the tone in the beginning, asking basic questions.
• "What actually happened?"
• "What physical sensations do you remember?" (Stretching, balancing, tension, strength.)
• "Any particularly interesting shapes or designs?"
• "Did you have any images?"
• "What was the most important moment?" (This specifically relates to the issue of form in improv.)
• "Does anyone have something you want to tell us about what's just happened?" (A more general opener.)

Guide the discussion but don't offer an opinion or evaluation, at least not until the movers themselves have talked about it from their point of view. After all they were the ones on the inside doing it.

Be aware that some groups jump in and talk with little encouragement; others hesitate with downcast eyes. If such an attitude persists, try preceding the group discussion by a short period of conversation between partners. Then bring the group together and try to elicit comments from them as a whole. When you need to save time (and don't particularly need the verbal feedback yourself), have them talk in pairs without meeting as a group. This still allows them a time to objectify and articulate the process and get some feedback.

What about directing the discussion toward the specifics of the improv?

Yes. The leader can use the structure, content, and parameters of the improv as the basis for investigation. For example, in an improv on sculpting, raise issues of design and three-dimensionality, of being active or passive, and of the variety of ways used to achieve sculptural changes in one's partner.

We seem to get bogged down on "how it felt." How can I get them to talk about less subjective issues?

After discussing "how the improv felt," direct attention to developing objective awareness. Some questions to assist this would be:
- "Do you remember any of the movement?"
- "How do you think it looked from the outside?"
- "Could you do the movement again? Try it."
- "There was a lot of traveling; what path did you take?"
- "Were there any distinctive shapes or ways of relating?"
- "If you were a quick sketch artist and had to draw one picture of the improv, what image would you pick and why?"
- "Did the improv have a distinct overall structure? Can you plot it out?" (Only ask this if indeed it did.)

Believe it or not, sometimes I have someone who talks too much.

Yes, sometimes a person will detail every little event at great length. Simply and politely indicate that it is not relevant to go into such detail, that it is someone else's turn, or that it is time to move again.

Do you always have to have discussions?

No.

I often slip movement concepts into the improvs, but I don't know if it is registering with them beyond the experiential level. Does this matter? How can I assure it's happening without seeming pedantic?

It does help to make the concepts explicit, and doing so can be fun. Below is a list of movement concepts that are usually covered by a beginning class. Present the list and have the movers make the words into pictures. Some possibilities are shown in figure 1.

(Note: Be sure they have already experienced the concepts in movement; otherwise it is just words, and who cares? You can, of course, add and subtract from this list to fit your own lesson plans.)

tempo: slow / fast

levels: low / middle / high

amount of space: lots / little

relating to others

stillness

scatter / gather

abrupt / sustained

energy: strong / gentle

impulse and follow through

body shape

straight and curved paths

turning, twisting

natural phrasing

even and uneven rhythms

endings

shaping the space

symmetry / asymmetry

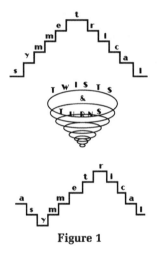

Figure 1

This is not a major study of the concepts, but it does encourage verbal awareness of movement. It can open discussion on the concept, and may stimulate the group to remember questions they had during the improv. If you do not want to take the time to do it in class assign it outside.

What about lesson plans?

Once the goals of the course are identified, choose the improvs accordingly. The plan for each lesson should remain flexible, ever responsive to changing conditions and to the participants' behavior as well as to redefined needs and goals. The degree to which lesson plans are used varies enormously from teacher to teacher. The personal style and pedagogy of the leader will determine their use.

What are the considerations in planning a series of improvs?

Since some experiences need to come before others, the sequence of improvs over a term should not be random. Each improv contributes to overall development and builds on those which have gone before. The issue is not only whether the movers enjoy the improv experience and get involved, but also whether a given improv maximizes its potential and contributes to long-range objectives. Would it be more productive if put in sequence with something else? Was it properly prepared for, and how can it be used as a springboard for other explorations? Random improvs can be fun, but so can ones which play a part in the larger picture—a two-day workshop or an entire term. So why not take the factor of developmental progression into account and get extra mileage out of the entire series?

What about building a session or series of sessions on a single theme?

Good idea. It gives a focus and ties the improvs together. The nature of the theme doesn't matter. You can create your own improvs for it or adapt existing ones. Frontier, for example, calls to mind large spaces, work rhythms, the floor patterns and relating of square dancing, the group unity needed for barn raising. Or use the time category in chapter 14, "Sources," as a starting point, including a mix of structures, formats, individual, pair and group work.

Can you suggest any other guidelines for determining the appropriateness of an improv?

Consider the following: the makeup of the group (age, level, identity, etc.), the amount of trust and depth of intimacy called for, the complexity of movement elements, the degree of risk involved (physical, emotional, interpersonal), the level of abstraction, the multiplicity of concepts being addressed.

When planning a whole course, what should I try to include?

Depending on your objective, you can think of the following as useful for incorporation daily, weekly, or over the course of the term:

(1) a mix of solo, pair, or group work; (2) a balance of abstract and concrete stimuli; (3) a variety of formats; (4) exploration of pure movement, dramatic intention, props, and environment.

Another suggestion is to use the different categories in chapter 14, "Sources," as a guide to insure breadth and depth of content.

Can you have a mixed group of beginners and advanced improvisers?

Certainly. Advanced movers can always do a lot with simple improvs, and to some degree they will carry the beginners along, their involvement accelerating the involvement of the beginners. But the situation is not ideal for either group. If possible (especially if the situation will exist over a long period of time) each group should be homogeneous.

If people come in late, should they be allowed to enter the improv?

If it is a group improv, no, let them watch. It takes time for a group improv to gel and form an identity; introducing a new person midway can be disruptive. An exception to this might be if she is a regular member of the group with a high level of sensitivity and good improv skills. If it is independent work, only just begun, and you believe she is experienced enough to get warmed up and connected, then fine, allow her to enter. Make your judgment based on the individual person and the specific improv. Remember too that observers learn a great deal.

Someone sat out last week and was so enthusiastic about watching that now everyone wants to watch.

You can accommodate that by allowing everyone time to watch. Or you can divide the class in half or thirds and allow each group to watch for a while. Observers make invaluable contributions to the discussion. Their excitement about how it looks from the outside is contagious, and invariably the experience aids their intuitive objectifying skills when they rejoin the group.

What should I do if someone always moves in the same way?

For starters, accept it. Telling him to stop or do something else simply will not work; gradually widening his range of movement may. With this approach, you can start with where he is and move him away, one step at a time. An important first step is when *he* can distinguish if he is in his rut or not. As you gradually introduce more changes, you hope he will respond to the challenges and vary his movement style.

If you feel the student can handle a more direct approach, have him identify the hallmarks of his style, perhaps in terms of qualities or affinities to time, space, or energy. Start with one of these and, keeping other aspects constant, gradually shift toward the opposite. For example, you may have a dancer who is a beautiful and lyric mover, but that's it; there's no variety. Start with where he is.

Away from Lyric

Dance some easy curves. Let's keep these curves but notice that the space is getting thicker, offering resistance. Carve the curves, using all parts of your body to do so. The movement doesn't flow so easily; it takes a great deal of strength. Let you body stabilize you to give you power. Feel the air turning frigid and hard. You find that the curves are sharpening into angles; carve them in the solidifying wall of wind. Include the weight of your body to make a deep impression in the stone, then larger obtuse gashes, using only isolated body parts: back, hip, shoulder. Continue using your entire body or isolated parts.

Concern for widening a movement style should be balanced by a cultivation of individual differences. Strategically placed comments will help bring awareness of individuality to a conscious level. "Did you see how Jimmy dove right in and attacked the center while Alex stalked around the edges checking out the situation?" Through your encouragement, the mover will come to recognize and value the uniqueness of each individual.

What do I do when the group is lethargic?

Is it exam week? Are all-nighters a fact of life? Perhaps this is the time to serve their needs by offering a class in relaxation techniques. Most often the solution is to instigate active, energetic movement and once you get them going, they'll keep moving.

What if they simply don't respond?

First make sure they can hear you—acoustics in a studio with a high ceiling can be atrocious. Then try repeating some of the instructions. Make them more movement oriented; vary the image. If appropriate, bring in a strong dramatic idea to stimulate a response or give more choices within the original context.

If that doesn't work, try the opposite; narrow in. Be directive. Take one possibility of the original idea, and make that the only choice. "Do this." After they are moving, lead an exploration all around it. As movement is generated you can again open up more choices.

Often in your desperation to get the group responding you will come up with more potent images and more logical sequences than when you are sitting at home making lesson plans. Thankfully the pressure of thinking on your feet often produces great results.

What about when an improv is not turning out?

Don't stop it unless it is not working on any level and even then, don't just stop abruptly. Realize the implications this may subconsciously raise for future work: "We didn't do it *right*. We weren't doing what *she wanted*." Instead, use the options of rephrasing, redirecting, stirring it around as you try to coddle it to health. However, know when enough is too much and try to bring it to a quick but graceful end. "How fast can you do the movement that you are doing? Go as fast as you can and end." In an extreme situation it may even mean bringing it to an unsatisfying conclusion. If that's the case, end quickly and simply and either discuss it or go on to something else.

Is there a checklist I can use if things are not working well in a specific improv?

Sure, try this one.

• Was time allowed for the people to center themselves and become neutral?

• Did you choose clear, movement-oriented words for the instructions?

• Did you encourage use of individual body parts as well as total use of the full body?

• Were the movers reminded of the space, time, and energy possibilities that the improv holds?
• Was the content and amount of structure appropriate and clearly given?
• Was the experience of the group equal to the level of sophistication of the instructions in terms of abstraction, forming, and relating?

You may also want to check for problems of a more general nature.

• Has trust in you, the group, the situation, and themselves been adequately established?
• Are there individual problems that you might not have dealt with, a personality type annoying others or some dissatisfaction that you have not attended to?
• Is the physical environment conducive to working?
• Where are they coming from before your session? Are they—as a group or any individual in it—tired, upset, or hyper?
• Are your purposes at odds with theirs? Are you too objective for a group that really wants a subjective, therapeutic session, too dramatic for postmoderners, or too physically demanding for old people?
• Is your style too obtrusive, aggressive, or laid back? Does it reflect a genuine interest in the group and in improvisation as a phenomenon?
• Do you have unrealistic expectations for the group? Are you imposing or waiting for specific things and therefore putting down original or tangential ideas?
• Is the subject of the improvs varied enough or does it repeat itself and therefore not challenge the group? Or do the improvs skip around too much, not allowing enough in-depth exploration and thus creating a feeling that things are superficial and scattered?
• Are you careful about intruding on privacy or sensitive issues?
• Are you careful about playing favorites?
• Are there problems with relating that have not been attended to?

If you have trouble gaining a perspective on your own work you can have the members of the group write up anonymous evaluations. While giving you a picture from their side, it can also help them become a bit more conscious (on a conceptual level) of the improv process. You can leave it open-ended, asking them to "address the course, content, yourself, leader, and/or peers." In this way they choose what is pertinent for them and tell about it in their own way.

What are some of the things I can build into group improvs that will help insure group unity?
• Start in a formation where physical relations are already established—a circle holding hands, a line, a huddled mass.
• Give a simple repeatable movement pattern that provides a common ground for everyone to do together, before tangents tease them away and individuals assert themselves.
• Define spatial parameters that encourage relation, for example, "Mill around within two inches of each other."
• Give images or request direct actions that cause relating: "Focus on someone's chin or ankle." "Make eye contact" (from nearby or across the room). "Touch palms or other parts as you pass." "Carry or lift someone."
• Provide simple rhythms which serve as a unifying force. Rhythm can keep a large group of people together even if they cannot see each other. (Once a group has experienced the power of the unity of rhythm, it will often reappear.)

For basic information on relating see chapter 2, "The Experiential Body of Knowledge," and chapter 14, "Sources" (especially the categories Self to Important Other and Self as Part of the Group).

I have worked for a term with this group. Overall I am pleased and they work well, but since we'll be continuing I want to look beyond and challenge myself further as a leader. What specific yardsticks can I use to evaluate our progress?
• How is this group different today than it was six, eight, or twelve weeks ago? Consider the level of trust, risk-taking, honesty of response, kinesthetic sensitivity, timing.
• Is their ability to concentrate deepening?
• Have they developed the capability to keep the improv going, to play the movement as it comes out, to build on momentum?
• Are they willing to devise and follow their own offshoots? Are these offshoots connected to the group as a whole? Are they valid to the topic and focus? Are they constructive?

- Is spontaneity becoming familiar and natural?
- Are they shedding their mannerisms and/or conventional dancer's movements in favor of original creative work?
- Have they begun to develop a sense of the internal observer?
- What has happened to awareness of each other's physicality and spatial needs?
- What changes have occurred in the ways in which they respond to the unexpected?
- Is their participation contributing to their own and each other's growth and development?
- To what degree are people contributing to the discussion (especially by comparison to earlier in the term)?
- What about the nature of the discussions—are they contributing to the understanding of the improv process and to the relationships between members as well as simply reporting what happened?
- Is there any one person who could use some individual attention? If so, who and how?
- Who are the natural leaders? How have others been encouraged or structured to also experiment with assuming those roles?
- Is someone consistently left out? If so, why? What can be done about it? What have you already done about it? What changes has that led to?
- Consider control and freedom—are they both being put into action appropriately?
- Are more sophisticated aspects and a greater variety of time, space, energy, and forming factors being automatically applied? Are these becoming intuitive?
- Overall, have there been opportunities for a variety of content and types of responses, including the dramatic, comic, pretty, distorted, silly, painful, calm, tense, cerebral, abstract?

6 Formats

Following are the four most widely used formats used by leaders in presenting improvisations; each has its own particular advantages.

Continuous Feed-in

In this format, instructions are given throughout the improv. At first the leader only says enough to get people started: initial awareness, focusing, and movement guidelines. As the movement progresses, the leader sees what is happening and accommodates his next instructions accordingly. It is important to keep the movement going while new directions are being inserted. At first, people unused to this method may stop each time you speak. A gentle reminder to "keep moving as I talk and incorporate the new instructions when you are ready," suffices. (Many of the improvisations that appear in the text use the continuous feed-in format.)

Advantages

• The leader can capitalize on the movers' unique reactions, by qualifying details, changing directions, adjusting the timing.
• Giving one new instruction at a time heightens immediacy, limits undesirable intellectualization, and eliminates the need to remember too many things at once.
• The leader (on the basis of his objective external assessment) can offer content or structural input at opportune moments.

Prestructured

By the Leader

All instructions are given by the leader before the improv starts. Contingencies are touched upon briefly. Since there is no input during the course of the improv the leader can ask if there are any questions before it begins. The improv then takes place, with the ending determined in advance, ("finish after you have completed the last task"), or signaled in some way by the leader. Instructions need to be kept sparse and simple so they are easy to remember.

By the Group

The leader gives the focus for the forthcoming improv and the group then discusses its possibilities in a mental brainstorming session that precedes the physical brainstorming of the actual improv. This is a good time to give permission and encourage people to "yes, indeed, do that!" For instance, if presenting Contact, Lifting, Carrying someone may suggest, "besides not using our hands, we could use an intermediary such as a stick or leg warmer to do the lifting," or the possibility of resisting and assisting in the activity. This gives the participants a greater sense of investment in the content, because ideas about the material have been shared and reinforced.

Take care to keep the discussion short; you don't want to end up with a talk session instead of a movement improv. Before starting the improv, do a short recapitulation of the main points. After the improv, discuss how the concepts were explored and manifested. The before-and-after discussion is a good way to focus on specific improv skills which are the natural, but sometimes unconscious by-products of the act of improvisation. It makes the participants aware of specific options and emphasizes their implementation.

You can use this format to work on a participant's idea for an improv or on a specific problem that the group may be having.

Another useful application of this format is in a situation where the first language of the group differs from yours. It provides time to clarify slang terms, strange words, and phrases, possibly through an interpreter.

Advantages

• It gives greater freedom and responsibility to the individual mover; she can progress through the various stages of the improv at her own pace.
• It allows the movers to get clarification before the improv begins.
• In the group version, the participants add their ideas, thereby increasing their sense of ownership.

Demonstration

The leader teaches a skill or physically demonstrates a beginning shape, movement quality, phrase, or sequence of actions which provides the point of departure. Depending on the improv, the demonstration may be simply an example to clarify the qualitative nature of what is being sought, or it may be necessary for all the members of the group to learn to do it exactly as shown in order to be able to explore the material. The improv **Sun Worship I** is an instance where everyone starts with the same movement; (also see the section on manipulation in chapter 14, "Sources").

The initial sessions of Contact Improvisation, developed by Steve Paxton, are a good example of this format.[1] In it, certain physical patterns are to be used as starting places in order to learn specific "contact" skills. These are demonstrated by the leader (often with a partner). For example, the two will face each other, put the crowns of their heads together and, keeping a continuous point of contact, easily begin to move their heads around on one another like ball bearings. The leader then shows how the movement progresses, allowing neck, shoulders, back, and so forth to become involved, with the rest of the body following simply in a mutual give and take of body weight. The initial placement of the heads is clearly shown and all the participants begin in this same specific way. The movement that ensues is determined by the partners' sensitivity to shifts of weight, leanings, lines of direction, pull, flow.

Advantages

• Everyone understands or has tried the required skill when the improv starts.
• Everyone starts with the same movement.
• It provides a bridge between rote imitation and complete freedom.

---

[1]For more information see the journal *Contact Quarterly*, which focuses on Contact Improvisation, improv in general, and on various Body Works. (P.O. Box 603, Northampton, Mass., 01061.)

Open Content and Structure

In this format, the objective is free and open-ended movement exploration. No content is imposed; there may or may not be an external stimulus, such as music. The movers progress until they individually reach a conclusion or until some external determinant calls a halt. The open content format is suitable for either a group or a solo, with or without a leader/observer. Or the leadership role may rotate among members of the group.

Authentic Movement, a form of movement exploration taught by Janet Adler Bottinger since 1971, uses this format. Although a leader or "witness" is present as an objective external eye, the choice of content remains with the individual movers. They are told to find a space of their own, close their eyes, and wait for a kinesthetic impulse. Attention is paid to heightening one's awareness of the physical sensations coming from within one's body (anything from a tension spot to a feeling of heaviness or an itch) and then allowing movement to occur naturally. The leader calls the end of the time period based on her sense of individual needs within the group.

Advantages

• When used with a single improviser, it gives complete control and responsibility to the individual.
• When used by a group it encourages a greater sense of collective self-sufficiency and determination.
• It fosters inner listening and kinesthetic awareness.
• It is completely inner-determined.

Every leader and group will find one approach that works best for them, but it is good to experiment with the others from time to time. This offers variety to the movers and helps keep the leader from falling into a rut.

7 Music

Music and dance are sister arts; both are temporal, relying heavily on phrasing, rhythm, and form. Having co-existed for a long time, there has been much cross fertilization. Most dance is performed to music, and many musical compositions were written specifically for dancing—allemande, waltz, disco, ballets—or to meet the specifications of individual choreographers.

Improvisation is done both with and without music and there are good reasons for either choice. Those leaders who automatically use music as background or stimulus for improvisation often cite its motivational aspects and rhythms. They are excited by the images which music can foster, as well as the variety in style, period, and ethnic input that wise music selection can offer. Furthermore there are fine compositional forms to be found in good music which can guide and structure the movement experience. On the other hand, this very capacity can deprive the mover of certain initiatives, such as determining phrasing, timing, and overall structure. And it is exactly this aspect which the advocates of improv without music see as detrimental, particularly for beginners. Besides taking the source of movement away from movement, they say it hampers individuals from relying on their inner resources, energy, curiosity, and creativity.

Music has its own persistent logic. It neither interacts with nor responds to the mover's individualized pursuits, but forges ahead on its own track. It may be furiously building while one or more of the dancers might have been more honestly concerned with continuing a meandering exploration. Not only can music influence the quality of movement response and the form, but it can also dominate the mover's perception and images. The following improv makes this apparent. Do it three times: the first time in silence; the second and third, using two very different kinds of music.

Becoming
You are neutral, zero, a nonentity; as you move, you become defined. Different aspects clarify, and small points become articulated. You can become anything from a specific person, animal, or character, to an embodiment of an idea or place, to an interplay of light and energy.

After all three improvs are finished, discuss the different kinds of things that were created and how they were influenced by the music.

As you review the improvs in this book which do not specifically call for music, notice how its addition would change both the structure and content. Notice, too, that it would hamper the use of the continuous feed-in format when leading and cause conflict between the timing called for by the mover's responses and that of the structure and authority of the music. Traditional Western European music has a strong mathematical-logical component that influences how one sound relates to another, building an internal structure of relationships that result in an overall form. Sounds in their relation to each other obey different laws than movements do. Harmonies, key changes, and so forth are building blocks of traditional music. There is something rarified and inevitable about the logic of music that is not present in the sweating, gravity controlled, momentum-hungry movement of the human body.

On the other hand, music can help find and guide new experiences. Personal rhythms can sometimes become pretty simplistic and overly repetitive, as can tempo and style. Wisely selected music can be used to open new doors and push people beyond the familiar and comfortable.

Consider the place and use of music in today's world. Music has come to be rampantly (and indiscriminately) present in our culture. We have radio, Walkman, TV, and Muzak. We are bombarded with it; we wake up, work, drive, jog, and relax to it. Music follows us down the grocery aisles and across the department store; it waits for us in our car, on the streets, and on the beaches. Our bodies, in fact, are so "in tune to" and "turned on by" the ever-present pop music sounds that it's easy to predict the sorts of physical responses one of the Top 40, with its heavy rhythmic base, will provoke. Being the customary dance music of the age, most people in improv classes have already acquired a semipatterned movement vocabulary which such music automatically calls forth. The tempo, quality, rhythms, and timbre are well known even if the specific song is not. Popular music is great for some things, but it takes an experienced and an exceptionally sophisticated improviser to ignore the habitual movement response it evokes and to play with, against, and around its all-consuming beat and idiom.

So, at least with beginners, let's delete popular music from our Music for Improv library. Instead, when we choose to use music, let's select from a wide range of periods and composers: Gregorian chants and Renaissance dances, the Baroque masters (from Bach to Mozart), the Romantics (Beethoven, Chopin, Schumann), the Impressionists (Debussy, Ravel), the twelve-tone scale innovators (Schoenberg, Stravinsky), the New Music group (Berg, Bartok), the Chance and Electronic schools (Brown, Cage), and the Minimalists (Glass, Reich).

Remember that the more familiar the music, the greater the chance that the response will be automatic and the harder it will be to get to original individual movement. Therefore, add music from other cultures; because of its unfamiliarity it will be more likely to foster the discovery of internal (and less habitual) aural-kinesthetic associations. Use the music of the gamelan, or Rumanian panpipes; try African rhythms, Eskimo throat-singing, Polynesian lullabies, environmental and mechanical sound recordings. The Nonesuch Explorer Series has a full range of musical possibilities and is a good place to begin if your ethnic music library is limited.

Providing a variety of music within the improv experience can actually be a way of broadening the group's musical background. You can expose your people to music that they might never have previously chosen to dance to, or to listen to. You can also get them to work with music in ways that they would not have considered by themselves. Choose each bit of music you use with care and with an ear toward your intended purpose. Sometimes you might want to use music to support, or serve as a companion for, the fuller investigation of some idea you initially worked on in an improv without music.

Besides providing a driving energy, supporting specific images, and introducing new movement experiences, music can help with certain movement problems. If, for example, you notice that people are repeatedly doing a series of short sections or are having difficulty with transitions, try some of Vivaldi's pieces that so brilliantly flow from one phrase into the next. Let the group listen and then move to the music, trying to catch and follow this flow.

If there's a glut of lyrical, pretty, flowery movement, challenge it by using unpretty, discordant music. If you notice that phrasing is fairly regular, select some piece that has a wide range of phrase lengths and have them follow the musical phrasing (Barber, Ravel, or Hindemith). If there is a narrow range of dynamics, play a Mahler symphony (for example, his fifth, which runs the gamut from delicate to heroically powerful) and ask them to move correspondingly. In these ways you use the music to achieve your ends.

Being musically astute adds one more refinement and skill to an improviser's bag of tools. Such knowledge has more to do with learning how to listen, and how to discern musical elements than with being able to identify the name and composer of major works. One excellent method for getting to know a new piece of music, or of rediscovering a known one, is by focusing attention first on one aspect—underlying beat, melodic line, atmosphere, or a particular instrument—and then on another. Do small improv snatches with the same section of the music, attending to one of these elements and then another and see how differently they develop. This is very valuable work for a choreographer who intends to use a specific piece of music. It is also a wonderful tool for a music theory class for dancers.

Music can also be used as the kick-off point rather than as accompaniment. Choose some music, dance to it, and see what kind of movement it leads to. Use the results as the basis for the theme or style of an improv. Give that improv to your class *without the music*. Repeat the improv with the original music. Get responses on the two improvs. Explain the origin of the improv. (See **Toward a New Jazz Style** in chapter 9, "Advanced Challenges," for a detailed way to use a specific style of music.)

For a challenge that isolates and focuses on a certain area of movement, select a piece of music that epitomizes the *opposite* of what you want to work on, such as random, abrupt music to contrast to sustained movement. Have the group consciously work *against* the music's style, timing, mood, or form. This approach is difficult and requires some finer improv skills, since before one can successfully counter something, one first has to be capable of clearly identifying and working with it. Thus you might want to consider using this improv only with experienced movers. (It also could be a very successful way to induce schizophrenia, cause frustration, or produce comedy, especially if you make a play of going in and out of working with and against the music.)

You can also investigate musical form through improv. First choose some music and determine its overall form. Let the structure of the music determine how you will organize the improv instructions or a combination of choreographed movement and improv. If you are using choreographed material, set one or two sections for the number of people in your group or some small grouping thereof. The choreographed sections can be in unison or interactional; they can consist of specific steps or simple directions. Teach these set parts. Be sure you set the group's formation and place in the room. Have them listen to the entire piece of music a number of times. Then give them improv instructions for the remaining sections, having them move with sensitivity to the music's structure and transitional elements.

Some music might allow a series of improvised solos, while the group is given a basic, low-key intention (for example, "Take the entire time to cross from upstage left to upstage right").

If the music has distinct thematic material that repeats periodically, set a phrase of movement (or a certain idiosyncratic type of movement) for that section only and repeat it or a variation, whenever the theme appears, improvising the rest of the time.

You can also work with the music's main climax—how is it prepared for and resolved?—and other aspects of the form such as repetition, question-response. Finally, you can give one movement motif to be manipulated to the music. (See the section on manipulation in chapter 14, "Sources.")

You can expand your use of music enormously by using live musicians. They can work with composed music, simply adding the vitality of live music to the improv experience, or they themselves can improvise. When the music is improvised, it opens an even richer territory. Here is a real opportunity for mutuality and interaction as the dancers and musicians play off each other.

Jazz musicians are obviously a natural for dance improv, since improvisation is basic to their idiom. The important thing is to get musicians who are truly interested not only in playing for dancers, but in participating in a give and take experience with them. The brilliant collaboration of musician Bill Dixon and the postmodern dancer/choreographer Judith Dunn was just such a partnership.

When working with musicians don't be shy about stating what to you may be the obvious: "We're hoping you can watch us and respond, as much as we can listen and respond to you." It's best to get this clear from the start.

Some basic ideas for working with a musician are:
• Have a music/dance conversation.
• Follow the leader (reversing roles).
• Agree on a form or an idea and work together to make it happen.
Here are some less basic ones:
• Have the movers physically interact with, on, over, around, under, or through their partnered musician(s). (This was done in *Someone Missing* by Margie Gills.)
• Have the dancers watch the musicians while they play their instruments and use their actions as the starting point for movement.

One last experience not to be missed is that of switching roles. At least once, try having the musicians move and the dancers create the sound. It's a risk for everyone, but lots of fun. And remember, when we're talking about sound or accompaniment, that includes standard instruments, constructed sound makers, standard instruments played nonstandardly, noninstruments (whirling hangers), voice, and body-made sounds.

The more you work collaboratively with musicians, singers, and other artists the more you will learn about underlying principles of the arts and how they transform from one medium to another. This leads not just to greater range in movement improvisation, but to a deeper understanding of aesthetics and the range and relationships of art forms.

In using music for dance improv the bottom line is to respect the music. Use it for a purpose and let it add to the experience; don't use it as an incidental decoration, a numbing background, or taskmaster.

(See the section for choreographers in chapter 12, "Specific Populations," for ways to use improv in set choreography. The examples there are to be used with music. Also check the unit on accompaniment in chapter 14, "Sources," for other possibilities.)

8 Create Your Own Improv

How is an improv built? How do you go from your initial idea, or goal, to presenting an improv that fulfills it? How do you capture your idea in words and build a structure which will incorporate it?

The process of developing instructions for an improv is similar, in part, to what happens when an experienced mover responds in an improv. Intuitive and physical responses serve the organizing and refining drive of our aesthetic sensibility which edits and shapes both the process and the product.

Basically the route traveled during an improv is:

Words (instructions) act as triggers to the creative consciousness stimulating a movement response. This movement metaphor either stays on the pure response level or gets overlaid with felt thought, movement images, ideas, or associations (which may or may not get captured in words), which in turn act as new triggers to the creative consciousness producing new movement.

We make a distinction between felt thought and word because often the sense of a movement does not materialize into an actual word. The felt thought itself will often act as the stimulus for more movement; therefore, this circle of response may continually regenerate.

When you design an improv and create the instructions, much of what goes on is the same, although the order is different:

The stimulus may first come in the form of a felt thought, a movement or movement concept. Words might arrive immediately or may come through our creative consciousness as we try the movement or idea out in our bodies. (Even if we don't move outwardly but just wiggle inside our skin, we are subliminally responding to our improv idea, testing out directions, tangents, free-associating in incipient movement and felt thought, and considering structures as we test it against and filter it through our movement experiences and improv-making knowledge.) All this information transforms into and finds expression in *words* which are the triggers to communicate the improv *instructions*.

Of course, the instructions need not be given in words. After all, one could say, "The instructions for the improv are . . . " and then slowly collapse to the floor, or run in circles, or simply look up. This is not a demonstration, but a nonverbal synopsis of content or theme.

THE STIMULUS

Ideas for an improv can come from a movement concept (Laban-analysis, choreography, dance theory, dance history); from any movement seen, done, remembered, or imagined (dance or not); from an intellectual concept which challenges you to find a movement equivalent; from seeing a social event that begs to be distilled to the purity of an improv; from hearing a story; from a daily event, personal interaction, mathematical theory, practical necessity; from the lines of a building or the rush of a river; from a soccer game, a mystery plot, the cracks on the wall, or a subway ride. Almost everything has been, or could be, successfully adapted for improvs. What you start with is far less important than what you do with it.

WORKING WITH THE STIMULUS

After you have picked your stimulus, decide what intrigued you: its movement possibilities? its emotional power? its great range of subtle distinctions? its inherent, far-flung tangents? its implied structure? its potential for paradox? If the original stimulus is an actual movement consider why you want to build an improv about it: is it the funny shifts of direction and focus? or the juxtaposition of weight and elevation? This is an important step since the stimulus can be developed in various ways.

Free associate on the stimulus. Allow images, feelings, movement qualities, symbols, spatial or temporal concepts, specific events, or past experiences to randomly roam the landscape of your inner eye.

For the moment, you need do nothing more with these; they will come up as needed to add dimensions or possibilities.

If you are not using a movement theme directly, you will need to find the movement aspects of the stimulus. This is more easily done for some ideas than for others. Some possibilities are: death—slowing down, weakening, calming, shriveling, anticipating; discarded candy wrapper—being crumbled, then blown in the wind; homework—burdened with heavy weight, carrying a load on your shoulders, wanting to break free.

As you work with the stimulus you may want to ask yourself some of these questions.
• Do you want to pinpoint movement in one particular part of the body? (*Destruction:* heel of hand, foot)
• Is locomotion a central consideration? (*Elevation:* in place and traveling)
• Are there specific design elements necessary to explore the image? (*Balance:* symmetry)
• Does it need to start in a particular position? (*Birth:* curled up)
• Or in a specific place in the room? (*Coming out:* in a corner)
• Are there any technical pointers or common sense reminders that would make realizing your instructions easier? (*Attacks:* take time to recoup between different series of attacks)
• Do you need to color or intensify the experience? (*Exits:* the exit tunnel is tiny and full of obstacles)
• What metaphors or examples from other art forms can you use? (*Lines and circles:* Calder's stabiles and mobiles)
• What other actions or images should you connect with the initial one? (*Friendship:* physical trust, being silly together)
• What related symbols come to mind? (*Death:* a cross)
• Does it naturally seem to call for a solo, duet, trio, small or large group? Or will it incorporate groups of different sizes as it progresses?

While the improv should have a single strong focus, other concerns can be incorporated. For example, an improv may be about five people working as a unit, but it can also explore traveling, a specific use of energy and floor patterns.

You should always keep in mind the particular nature of the group you are working with. You'll constantly want to tailor your instructions to their level of experience, age, orientation, and needs. (These considerations are so critical that we've devoted a chapter to some specific ones; see "Specific Populations.")

Do you have a specific goal for this improv? Is it part of a series leading to relating? Is it to get the movers introduced to, and well versed in, the various aspects of a particular movement quality? Will it begin with individual exploration and lead to group interaction? Your intention will influence the image you choose and the way you develop the instructions. Of course, it is possible to have one improv idea serve a number of intentions (see chapter 12, "Specific Populations," where we use a basic improv, Journey, and change it to meet different intentions).

STRUCTURING THE IMPROV

Now you need to structure the improv, to give it form. Your idea may have a clear starting place (birth) with an unknown destination, or you may know where you want to arrive (a huddle in a corner) so that in planning the instructions you work backward, establishing a bed of experiences and a progression that will lead to the desired end. Other times the idea (separation) is the center and you have to reach back to get the movers grounded (begin together), and forward to completion (each one alone).

Progressions of any sort serve to organize material. They can go from simple to complex, literal to abstract, private to public. You can use progressions in their own right or impose one on other material, such as a story. Usually progressions can move in either direction, as in chaos-to-order or order-to-chaos.

When people are improvising the improv often takes on a specific dynamic shape. Commonly it starts quiet and small, then gradually builds to a high point which resolves to something more contained. There seems to be a certain dynamic inevitability. The tendency toward this shape has physical and psychological origins. When people improvise, there is a natural inclination to explore the possibilities tentatively before gradually committing themselves to a movement, an idea, or a relationship. Once a connection is made and you begin to focus on particular material, you push limits, break boundaries, find new extensions, and reach a peak. This peak is not necessarily a peak of raw physical energy but one of intensity, maybe in terms of intimacy, or in complexity of movement. You stay with this exalted place for as long as it grows, then you push it one last degree, and almost on its own it goes over toward resolution, winding down, collecting itself. You tie up loose ends (tuck legs in, pull the last person into the tightly knit group). Finding yourself in a completely new place or returning to some aspect of the beginning, you polish the last design, make a final connection, take a deep breath and end.

As you can see, this shape is determined by the act of exploration and discovery as well as by the medium of human movement. After being curious, daring, and committed, we *do* get physically tired. We also reach a level of physical and intellectual satisfaction and emotional satiation. This is true for both the improviser-performer and the audience and is therefore a theatrically effective shape: present material, build excitement, and tie things together.

What is interesting to note is that this improv structure roughly follows the golden mean, the classical sonata allegro form and the Fibonaccian sequence (0,1,1,2,3,5,8,13,21 in which each term is the sum of the two preceding terms), in its approximate ⅔, ⅓ ratio. The universality of this internal organization is reaffirmed by the fact that these formulas are derived from different media (numbers and notes).

The following is a quote from a student's journal entry about the improvisation **Amoeba.** ("Form a tight unit and as a group move across the floor.") It is a good example of a group following rather simple instructions and coming up with this classic improv shape. "We started as a tight knit group moving across the room. We became involved in the fluctuating shape of the group. Somehow a rhythm started; we all moved to it and the group got tighter and started to move as a unit. We moved as with one mind (with amazingly abrupt changes). A main rhythm drove us. It took over, mesmerizing us, driving us. I didn't think we could go on, but we did; we had even more energy than before. Soon there were counter rhythms challenging us, blocking us, yet needling us on, actually unifying us in defiance. We started turning in the center like a whirlpool, increasing the speed and the cohesiveness of the group. Then we burst apart and scattered; we each found our own separate place, established our own sphere. We were connected with intermittent pulsing rays, each of us to everyone else; no one was lost but we were very far from each other."

Instead of starting with an idea you can start with the structure, a design, or a doodle and make it the overall form. There are many possibilities; for instance, there could be a number of short-lived explosions before final success, or there could be periods of relative quiet, interrupted by high activity. For other ways of conceiving a structure for an improv, you can borrow directly from classic musical forms such as AB, rondo, theme and variations. Here are some ideas for a structure that begins at a high point.

Beginning	Middle	End
1. Light, fast, travel	Light, slow, travel	Heavy, slow, in place
2. War: The final battle	The journey home	Home
3. Ecstasy-love duet	. . .	Settling in together
4. Dared!	Failed	. . .

CLARIFYING THE INSTRUCTIONS

There are a number of ways to direct the improvisers' exploration and make the experience richer. These techniques will clarify the theme while they also extend the possibilities inherent in the material. Let's consider an improv about *light, small, abrupt attacks* to illustrate.

• *Emphasize by contrast.* "Use large, strong sustained movement as a way to gather strength, or to get into a position for the next attack."

• *Use details and nuances.* "See how many variations of 'small' you can find. Vary the locations and directions. Keeping them all light, make some lighter than others. Vary the rhythm of the attacks; use different small parts of the body as the initiating agent or the target place."

• *Review.* After leaving something that was explored at length and going on to other experiences, allow the possibility of a return. "Let the attacks get larger, longer, and stronger so that they are initiated abruptly but then have a sustained follow-through. . . . Now see if the little abrupt attacks can return and decorate or interrupt the larger one with the sustained follow-through."

• *Use concrete images.* "It's a summer night and you're near a mosquito infested swamp." Or, "You have a sharp pin in a room full of balloons."

• *Change the point of view.* "Put yourself on the receiving end; you are being inundated by multiple tiny yet direct and dangerous attacks."

• *Change gradually to a contrasting quality.* "Keep the attacks small and abrupt but make them stronger, more powerful. Once the strength factor is achieved, allow a follow-through until it becomes sustained."

• *Define terms.* "Let the attacks be more explosive, more direct."

• *Set conditions and limits.* "Direct all the movement only sideways or behind you."

Depending on the situation and your goal with the group one idea can be presented in a number of different ways. Here is a single improv idea, **Journey,** that is articulated with increasing specificity, detail, and amount of leader input. (**Journey** is also used as the basic improv in chapter 12, "Specific Populations.")

Journey I
Go.

Journey II
Go on a journey.

Journey III
You are going on a journey. Let the journey begin. Include traveling. Something gets in your way. How can you get past it? Bring your journey to an end.

Journey IV
You are going on a journey. Find a place to start. Let a pulsing begin to move you. It radiates, spreading to other parts of your body. It starts to move you through space. Something gets in your way; it may be tangible (a person or a cliff) or not (a memory, a pain in your side). How can you get past it? Good. Now you can complete your journey. Go the last little way and bring it to an end.

Journey V

You are going on a journey. Take a few minutes to find a spot where you can settle and which will be your starting place. Imagine yourself in a small quiet space in which you are still. A tiny pulsing movement starts in one part of your body. It is restless; it travels to different parts of your body (maybe the original starting place keeps pulsing); the restlessness takes you into space. You realize it is taking you somewhere; are you going directly there or are you approaching it indirectly? In either case something gets in your way. What is the nature of the obstacle? Is it something small and distracting or is it large and actually presenting a physical hindrance? How does it alter or affect you? Bypass it, wrestle with it, or have it join you. Perhaps cajole or overpower it. You are almost at the end of your journey; go the last little way. When you get there, make a final movement statement with a consciousness of the circumstances you've dealt with along with way and bring your journey to an end.

In the above progression, more and more information is given that shapes this structure and defines the content. We are not saying that the last, most detailed version is the one to aim toward. It all has to do with what is right for the particular circumstances at the time, and only you can determine that. It is probably a good idea sometimes to give lots of very precise instructions and at other times to allow the movers great latitude. Such range in your input will gradually help the movers in their improvisational development.

ENDING

At some point you need to decide how far you want to take your improv and whether you will guide its conclusion or allow it to find its own. You can actually determine the end by creating physical necessities that propel the movers toward it: "Continue turning but let it get slower and lower, winding, down to the floor; there is less and less movement but there are still little gentle circles in isolated body parts, shoulder, finger, chin. Then these too die out."

Another possibility is to end the improv abruptly at a high point.

High energy endings, like beginnings, usually require conscious structuring. Encouraged by music with a powerful ending, choreographers often conclude their works with sustained exuberance. Clearly there is excitement in a grand finale, and theater audiences love it. While a solo improviser may spontaneously end abruptly at the highest point (the intensity bursting and leaving her with no more to do), it does not happen often. As a group dynamic it is even rarer.

Of course if you want to end an improv at a high point there are other choices besides a high burst of energy. Perhaps after a highly structured and ordered movement there could be chaos, a confusion or directions, qualities, and rhythms, scattering attention, shattering the former unity and order. On the other hand a previously diverse group could come together with one strong focus, streamlining all energies to one force.

See chapter 5, "Leaders' Concerns," for a discussion of endings.

EDITING AND PRESENTING

It takes time to refine an improv: think it through, write it out, edit it, dance it yourself, add images and take out redundancies. Then try it with your group, watch their movement responses, listen to their remarks, rework it. After all, language is a funny thing; words don't always mean to other people what they meant to you. Give the improv to another group allowing flexibility in your approach; try side roads. How was it different from the first group? Where were the different areas of exploration? emphasis? growth?

Careful presentation of the instructions, with an eagle eye for eliminating clutter and disruptive or off-the-track tangents helps to build cohesive experiences. Instructions can be multilayered as long as they broaden and deepen (not confuse) the central idea. Each successive image sharpens and refines the idea, adding overtones and stimulating unusual ways of responding. Sometimes these layers may be contradictory yet still serve the intention. Suggestions which run counter to the established mood can yield pertinent and useful results. Movers may relish the challenge of dream logic and be encouraged to get in touch with their own multifocus awareness as a trigger for multidirectional responses.

Above all, don't read your improv; it is not a speech. Reading is a one-way street from page to listener. It gives neither you nor the group the option of influencing the content, pacing, and so on. Actually, most of your best ideas will come as you are giving the improv, as you are responding to their movement or lack of it. You'll soon find you are meeting the needs of the group spontaneously, leading by the seat of your pants.

9 Advanced Challenges

When experienced improvisers have worked together for a long time, they develop an intimacy and cohesiveness which allows a richer exploration than is possible for beginners or even for a new group of skilled improvisers. However, along with their more sophisticated ways of dealing with the material, they may have also developed a fairly regular pattern or consistency of approach. This is as it should be, but then comes a time to redefine goals and move on to more complex issues. This process of continued growth should be as challenging for the leader as it is for the participants.

CHALLENGING THE MOVERS
Increasing Objectivity

Increasing the movers' ability to view the improv objectively, without diminishing the subjective aspect, refines their perception. It heightens their degree of mastery and control, thereby allowing further cultivation of risk. Responses will be influenced not only by what feels good, but by what contributes to the artistry of the event. By artistry we are referring to the improv's inherent aesthetic value manifested by elegance in form and content, and achieved by the subtlest melding of the intuitive and rational processes.

There are several ways you can help your group achieve a higher level of objectivity.

Re-creating
After any improv, recreate in your mind's eye what actually happened—not what it felt like. How did it look to the detached watcher? What form did it take? Give it a title. Get up and try to re-create a few of the moments in movement, possibly developing them in a way which adheres to the original intention without straining to recapture each and every movement. Teach part of it to someone.

106

Out and In Again
Using any improv structure, include the requirement that each
participant exit the improv at some point to observe, call in additional instructions, and then reenter.

Directing a Duet
Divide into threes. One person creates an improv that is specifically tailored to the other two. They improvise his structure as a
duet. As they move he gives them feedback about the way they are
responding, for example: "That's good; stay with it." "Don't forget
to . . . " "That may feel good, but it's so cuddly that it's not going
anywhere." "Uh-oh—that change was arbitrary. You just dropped
a developing movement idea; try to find its natural conclusion or
transition."

Discuss the improv and the verbal feedback. Were you able to
relate to the feedback? Was there enough? Too much? Did it get in
the way of your involvement with the movement? Did the leader
impose too much of his personality, expectations, or goals?

Repeat with another improv using a group of about five people
moving and one person giving feedback. "Keep awareness of the
entire group. That's a good shape—don't let it dissolve so quickly,
stay with it. Be aware of what Mark is doing; do you want to incorporate that?"

Repeat with no outside observer but with each member of the
group free to verbalize perceptions and concerns as they are moving, even stepping out for a minute to observe and comment.
This is a good way of heightening internal objectivity while the
activity is in progress.

Increasing Awareness of Others

While the members of an experienced group most likely are sensitive to each other and to the needs of the group, the following improvs will challenge them even further and allow them to refine this
skill.

Trading Focus
In two groups of two to ten people each, start a simple pattern to
establish a sense of group. Unison movement works well here (in

a circle, hold hands and sway), or use a simple rhythm to move toward and away from each other. Each group should have a different movement. Both groups begin at the same time and then they take turns as the focus of attention. When one group concludes its time in the imaginary spotlight, the other group will take the attention. Your awareness will be primarily toward your own group's ebb and flow, but you must maintain a keen sense of the other group in order to allow them their turn and to know when they are passing the focus on. When the focus is on the other group you don't stop moving; rather, you allow your movement to become subdued. It functions as background, not calling attention to itself. In some ways your group is in a holding pattern, but it could inch along to a different place so that when it starts up again it is ready with new material. How the focus gets passed has to be felt by each group, each time; there are no prearranged cues. The leader may want to indicate which group should start and help the first couple of transfers.

Discussion: What calls attention to a group? Some things are obvious: large jumps, high tension, speed, and dramatic intentions. Yet a strongly defined group, with clear and interesting designs and sustained slow movements, can be compelling enough to steal the focus from a group with high energy. How aware were you of the other group? How did you know when it was time to transfer? Was it easy? Why or why not?

This is a great improv to watch; you may want to have a few people sit out.

Multiple Focus
At random, choose any improv from the Self to Important Other category in chapter 14, "Sources." As you work through it, keep constant attention on the core of that improv while you also attend to one or more of the following: (1) your own transfer of weight; (2) the form of the entire piece so it could be drawn; (3) what one person in another pair is doing (with enough clarity so you can reproduce several moments once the improv is over).

Any number of other foci could be added or substituted, such as moments seen from your partner's point of view, recurring rhythmic phrases, and so on. Naturally, the more foci that are simultaneously layered in, the more difficult and challenging it becomes.

Dictated Conversation
In groups of three, have two people sit facing each other, carrying on a verbal conversation. The third person dances behind one of them so she is only seen by the person facing her. She pays no attention to the conversation. The person who sees the mover adapts content and emotional tone of his part of the conversation to her movements. It might be best to begin by having the person who sees the mover tell a dream or story with the other commenting and asking questions. Take turns with the different roles.

Variations: (1) the mover can hear the conversation and tries to guide it (she could have an intention in mind or one may develop according to the response she hears); (2) instead of talking, the couple is having a movement conversation; (3) one mover for all couple conversations (verbal or movement).

Changing is a good preparation for this improv.

A big challenge in increasing group awareness (for the working members and for the leader) would be to use very large groups.

For Fifty
Design an improv for fifty people. When working with large groups keep the content and structure simple. If you use the prestructured format, you can arrange signals (blinking lights, a drum beat) to do the internal cueing once the improv is in progress. Or consider giving general instructions to everyone and detailed instructions to only a handful of people, asking the rest of the group to be sensitive and responsive to what is happening. Be sure you allow plenty of time for exploring the instructions; there is a lot of accommodating and integrating that takes place with large groups. Even simple things take time to register across a field or gym. Try using music (recorded or live) for an excellent unifying device. Or have the movers hum, chant, or clap to produce a common rhythm. Use pure movement themes or explore the occasion for the gathering—a farewell, a welcome, or a celebration.

Culling and Editing

Looking at an improv in the following way will provide a keener and more sophisticated sense of its process, intention, and overall form. This exercise is good for the student of choreography.

Reduction

Think back to a distinctive improv you have done, one that was more than five minutes long. Can you show the essence of that improv in thirty to sixty seconds? Can you reduce it or make an abstract of it, a summary, an outline? What was distinctive about it—the form, the mood, or the dramatic interaction? The last two minutes might have produced the only worthwhile material. Or perhaps the progression from beginning to end was the mainstay of the piece, so you can reduce it by briefly touching each station along the way.

Do any solo improv. Reduce it. Do a duet improv; together discuss and reduce it. Do a small group improv; without discussion repeat it in reduced form.

Stretching the Boundaries of Style

Each person's movement style is a uniquely expressive signature. It includes mode of expression, execution, and construction, and is influenced by such basic elements as body structure (size and shape), type of training, personality, and willingness to commit the self in movement. Personal preferences also affect style: "I always connect to rhythm"; "I hate mushy, gushy, dramatic stuff"; "I always accommodate, it feels friendlier"; as do aesthetic affinities for pure movement, gymnastics, or narrative material. A person's style is defining but not limiting; it is a tendency from which to branch out. In movement the style of one's response is often a result of choices made some time ago. For instance, the style of dance one studies influences the way one moves. Studying dance is actually a process of inhibiting certain reflexes while preferentially honing others.

The following exercise is only for a group that has been together for a long time and which has a high level of trust, for it demands delicacy and support as well as critical observation.

Personal Style

As a group, take one person at a time and talk about what kind of movements he usually does, what you have never seen him do, what it is like to interact with him, and what his mode of response is in the improv situation. "Your face is beautifully expressive but often it takes over and your body movements seem passive, secondary"; "Each time we are in a group, at some point you circle around us a number of times"; "This funny twisting movement with the arm—you do it a lot"; "I have never seen you travel"; "You are very creative and I love to move with you, but it seems that I always enter your world; you never come to one of my making."

After allowing that person to respond and perhaps ask some questions, have the group make up an improv that will encourage them to pay attention to some of the issues stated. Pair off and do the assignments with one person looking on and giving feedback either during or after the improv.

Note that you are not seeking to change that person's style, just to direct his awareness during a specifically tailored improv. The assignment should encourage him to broaden his range by demanding a less automatic movement response, or encouraging a type of interaction which he seems to avoid: a movement conversation wearing a mask or an arm dance without any twisting movements.

Beg, Borrow, or Steal

Pick a piece of established choreography which has captured your imagination, but has a movement vocabulary decidedly different from your own. Identify the elements which constitute that style. For example, let's say that the movement you enjoy and usually use in improv and choreography is quite "dancey," and you saw a piece where movement was created from broken gestures, some identifiable, some barely so, some almost in the realm of tasks. Using this as a point of departure, you could make an improv for yourself which was limited to gestural and task-oriented movement that would be arbitrarily interrupted either by yourself or by some external source (for example, every time you see anyone turning, you stop whatever you are doing and immediately substitute a different gesture or task).

Another way to expand boundaries is to explore in depth one of the many styles of dance. Jazz dance now popularly used in music videos, musical theater, concerts, and night clubs is a perfect vehicle for this exploration. This will be especially challenging because the jazz dance vocabulary is both widely known and somewhat limited, and in many cases restricts itself to using only rock music.

This section should be used by those movers who want to broaden their range within the jazz idiom. We use the content and structure of jazz dance and jazz music, and the jazz culture as points of departure.

Toward a New Jazz Style
• Pick three different pieces of dance music (clog, Charleston, Twist), research the times and the dance style, then improvise in the spirit and without the specific steps. (See **In the Spirit but Without the Steps.**)
• Use typical tap music where there are spaces in the music for the taps, and have a rhythmic conversation with the music. Using all parts of your body, make the rhythm visible instead of audible.
• Work with a variety of jazz music (Fusion, Big Band, Old Dixieland, Progressive) using isolations of the body as the motivating kinesthetic force.
• Using blues music: (1) work with its energy and timing; (2) work with the idea and themes of the blues, with and without the music.
• Take five typical jazz dance positions. Put them in any order and use as a picture outline as you improvise your way from one to another. Do this without music.
• Take three typical steps from a jazz dance class and use them as a motif to be manipulated. (See the unit on composition in chapter 14, "Sources.") Try it without music; with jazz music other than rock; with rock.
• Analyze the movement style and thematic material of choreographers Jack Cole, Bob Fosse, or Alvin Ailey. Find music that they would use. Improvise "in the style of."

• Choose five movements from an African dance class; play with each one separately. Mix. Try with two different kinds of African music.

• Since the internal structure of jazz music (use of ensemble and solos, a development of a melodic theme, a progression of chord changes) plays an important part in a great deal of jazz music, study a piece and then improvise to the structure alone. Then try it to the music, still following the structure. Try it again paying attention to other aspects of the music. Once more just for fun.

• Identify some aspects of teen culture: dress, gestures, attitudes, dances, music. Use them to build an improv with or without appropriate music.

• Research any cultural-historical aspect of the development of jazz music and/or dance (the dance marathons) and create an improv accordingly.[1]

• What themes do you associate with the jazz culture—teasing, drugs, pimping, street life, broken hearts, new love, old love, exhibitionism, being cool, being hot? Use some to build an improv.

• Use rhythm. Depending on the sophistication of your group, use various exercises to develop their consciousness and skill in rhythms, both alone and as a means for interaction. Try different rhythms simultaneously in different parts of the body (a basic element in African dance). Identify some typical jazz rhythms and employ them as a basis for an improv. Get a jazz musician or a group to come and try it with them.

• See any of the performing dance companies that emphasize jazz. Watch critically for how they are or are not working innovatively within the jazz idiom. The Jazz Tap Ensemble and the American Dance Machine are strongly recommended.

• Invite some jazz musicians and have a good time.

---

[1]Suggested reading: Gus Giordano, *Anthology of American Jazz Dance* (Evanston, Ill.: Orion, 1975), and Marshall and Jean Stearns, *Jazz Dance: The Story of American Vernacular Dance* (New York: Schirmer Books, 1979).

Expanding Exposure

Encourage a variety of experiences which may jolt the group out of the usual and stretch not only their responses but their definition of dance improv itself.

Some projects are:
• Invite in a new leader with a different orientation (drama, therapy).
• Have each member of the group act as leader for a session or a single improv.
• Have a session with a local theater improv group or with jazz musicians.
• Create and put on a *community* improv for thirty-three to ninety-nine people.
• Develop a ritual around an established myth or some aspect of the group and keep refining it until you can show it.
• Invent an improv where three groups are given three different sets of rules to play the same game.
• Invite someone new to join the group for at least one day and devise an initiation.
• Invite three willing children to join in as participants.
• Improvise on the subway at three different stations.
• Everyone bring a friend.
• Do a series of improvs using nonverbal instructions: present a windup toy; do a movement sequence with a hand puppet or marionette; use a look of your eyes; use a seven-second video clip (sports, science, commercial, or news), rhythmically tap different parts of your body, blink, or throw a paper airplane.

Here are some other improvs and experiments which are more specific.

Cultural Heritage
In some parts of the world improvisation is regularly incorporated into folk dances: Hungary, Spain, India, Italy (tarantella), the Arab countries (belly dance, chain dance, and combat dance), Korea, and Africa (specifically among the Akan of Ghana and the Tiv of Nigeria). Invite someone in who performs and teaches the dance of one such culture. Have your group learn some basic steps, being sure to work on clarifying the movement style. Encourage

the teacher to explain the cultural context of dance—where and when it is done, who participates, who watches, what the appropriate boundaries of behavior are, what elements are improvisational and how they are structured.

Using the traditional music of that culture, put the steps together in different ways, improvising a variety of patterns; then begin to insert some other improv material keeping the spirit of the traditions. In many countries stories are told through an established alphabet of gestures; but *how* the story is told is improvised by the dancer. Try to create as much of the context as you can— costumes, vocal component, groupings, settings, and so forth.

Masks

Work with neutral masks, or with commedia dell'arte, African, Mexican, Balinese, or others. You can also make your own. Wearing a mask often yields a transformation; it may involve a ritual in donning the mask and be part of a sacred event. Once on, what does it allow: more exhibitionism? aggression? silliness?

Video/Dance

Do a duet for one camera and one mover. Or take turns being the cameraman for the moving group. Let the camera dance with its own movement; let it go to unconventional places—on the floor, upside down, and in the midst of the group. Or keep the camera stationary and concentrate on framing isolated parts of the body (fingers and inside of the elbow). For this and the following, make full use of the monitor for feedback. Try letting the mover take responsibility for the picture. Choreograph a repetitive movement for the camera and add an improvising mover. Make a dance/video.

Break-out

This improv requires an entire session and is done out of doors. Once the group leaves the studio and goes outside, no verbal communication is allowed. One at a time, each person takes on the leadership role and uses any technique or device to communicate his directions to the group. He is responsible for creating (1) an improvisational way to get the group to a new place where his improv will occur, and (2) the content and structure of that improv once they've arrived. Every member of the group is expected to volunteer to lead at some point, which means they must sense the conclusion of the current leader's section as well as their own readiness to take the lead.

Since this is a difficult improv try the following as preparation.
• Do a trial run, with the leader devising a series of two or three environmental improvs set up wordlessly. (Become statue figures in or around an outdoor sculpture, fountain, or garden.)
• Have the group do some instant verbal brainstorming on how an improv can be signaled and explained without language.
• Work through **Moving Focus** to heighten sensitivity in identifying conclusions.

Anti-Dance

Sometimes, instead of looking *to* dance for ideas, try looking *away from* dance. First make a list for yourself of the criteria that define dance. Then work against them.

For instance:
• If dance is visual, then do the improv in total darkness.
• If it is rhythmic, then use no rhythm.
• If it contains aesthetic elements, then do functional maneuvers.
• If it implies form, don't let a form develop (for example, cut off impulses and directions, or dissipate momentum by frustrating the accumulation of impulses or returning to a neutral stillness between each phrase, or have the leader randomly insert a task or an unformed movement pattern).
• If it takes place all at one time and in one place, then interrupt that unity (for example, wherever you are on Monday, Wednesday, and Friday at 9:17, improvise for exactly 1 minute and 27 seconds, thinking of these as one improv momentarily interrupted).

Finding anti-dance ideas often means simply identifying the assumptions that we have about what dance is and then denying or thwarting them in some way.

When you are working with an advanced group, you need not orient each improv toward a complex challenge. Experienced movers will most likely take an improv to new places, automatically providing their own challenges, setting goals or limits which by their very nature cause deeper exploration, wider tangents, or more off-the-wall responses: "I wanted to try it without letting myself do . . . " Therefore improvs for experienced movers range from quirky, complex, mind-and-body teasers to simple stimuli ("Hide!") to which they are assumed to bring new perceptions, skill, and daring.

To provoke these more advanced responses, you could preface a fairly simple structure with a discussion of how the material could be dealt with in advanced terms. Elicit ideas on how to make the improv more challenging personally.

Some of the things we see in the responses of experienced movers include:
• Crafting of movement resulting in elegant simplicity, unique complexity, integrity, and control.
• Having keen and extraordinary perceptions and interpretations of what is happening (both within themselves and from the perspective of the group as a whole), and capitalizing on these.
• Intuitively making aesthetic choices.
• Retaining a natural sense of ease in difficult circumstances, such as improvising in an unusual public place.

CHALLENGING THE LEADER

Just like their students, leaders too need to be challenged. Once you've found and established your modus operandi, it can and should develop into a safe, well-working system. Effective and successful as it may be, there are several reasons for taking the time to reassess it and, every so often, try something new. This is not dilettantism or change for the sake of change, but a way of keeping you interested, creatively active, in touch with your own growth. Occasional experimentation with new approaches or alternative procedures brings an edge of anticipation while it indirectly supports one of the overriding maxims of improv—that of ever exploring new paths.

Here are some ways to change the way you think and work as an improv leader.
• Take a dance improv class with someone else; preferably someone

with a different background or orientation. Be a participant in some of the improvs and an observer in others. Assess range and level of response. Note the ways and means the leader employs. How do they differ from yours? Which could you adapt? What skills do they focus on? Are they ones you neglect? What's the most valuable thing that the students seem to get from the experience?

• Take an acting improv class. Note differences of emphasis and technique. What's the goal of the leader? What approach is used? What sensitivities and skills do you see being honed? Even though the mediums are different, what is there in the structures, content, or approach that you can use?

• Talk with people who lead improvs of any kind—psychodramatists, therapists, jazz musicians, experimental singers, other dancers. Discuss their philosophy about improv both in concept and implementation. State some problem you have encountered as leader; ask how they would deal with it. Ask to observe one of their sessions, or invite them to yours. Talk afterward.

• Keep a journal of your own, including the improvs you have led, types of responses, significant results, clarifications, realizations. Note your tendencies, and avoidances. How much do you talk? Do you prefer concrete concepts, tasks, games, or emotional narratives? Do you always use music or do you religiously avoid it? Try a dramatic change of length, format, and type of stimulus. Notice the differences in results and how you feel about them. Which things would you like to nurture further?

• What are your yardsticks for excellence or success; are you leaving out anything which may be relevant? Review the checklist at the end of chapter 5, "Leaders' Concerns."

You'll notice that we are essentially asking you to do the same thing we encourage the movers to do—increase your objectivity, expand your style, vary experiences and response patterns, and work toward honing your skills. Your responsibility as a leader extends to all three components which make up the improv experience—the movers, the improv, and yourself as leader. The standards of flexibility, challenge, resourcefulness, and evaluation apply to all and need to be honestly and constantly renewed and pursued.

10 In Performance

The use of improv in performance is an intriguing yet precarious undertaking. It is chancy; all the things you not only forgive but cherish in an improv, because you are emphasizing the process, are not necessarily the same things that satisfy a paying audience in a theatrical setting. Yet superbly done, by masters of the art, there is nothing quite like it. Improv definitely does have its place in performance.

Why would anyone want to take part in, or watch, an improv performance? Even with experienced movers there is a risk; but the recognized gamble is itself part of the fascination for both performers and audience. Though an improv by definition emphasizes process, and performance by definition emphasizes product, here is one instance where process becomes product. It is exciting for the viewer to watch the process in action; there is an anticipation of the unexpected, the unknown. Improv has a raw intensity, a vital energy at work, an edge, an on-the-lineness, a balancing of passion and freedom with craft and control. For the performers the challenge is to capitalize instantaneously on what gets thrown into being, and to form, cultivate, and bring it to its fullest development. A strong, spontaneous group dynamic is as fascinating to watch as it is to be a part of. There is a shared urgency in its "one-time only" nature that can't be paralleled by any set performance. Of course there is no guarantee that all this adds up to great art; it is not sacred because it is raw process. But it is exciting and great things *do* happen.

Many things contribute to this event of disciplined spontaneity. Consider that the vocabulary of movement called upon in an improvisation is unquantifiable, simply because of what improv is— spontaneous, unknown. In regularly choreographed pieces, a given number of steps are rehearsed again and again. The specific technique required for the masterful execution of those movements is refined beyond the skill which would be found by any of the performing individuals in their day-to-day class work. This is true for superb dancers as well and constitutes one reason why people so often appear to dance better onstage than in the studio.

In improv, the dancer doesn't have this opportunity for refinement of a given set of known material. There's no way of knowing what will be called for in terms of strength, speed, flexibility, coordination, endurance, and balance (not to mention dramatic range, sense of humor, interpretation, and other nontechnical skills). Therefore improvisation-in-performance for the performer-artist is hardly easy. Quite the contrary. Each improviser must keep her body tuned to its utmost, without the luxury of being able to concentrate on the specific skills needed for any given dance or movement in a set repertory. Failure to keep a high standard of technique or movement access will show up in a limited range of movement available for the improv. This will force the improviser to make choices on the basis of what she is capable of doing and not on the basis of what is organically necessary for any given moment.

All committed improv performers worth their salt know that a movement incapacity sets limitations on their improv world. They work constantly to expand their performance capability and thus can create and meet the new challenges which they thrive on. Therefore they need not only strength and coordination but the kinds of movement facility that may come from unconventional sources— yoga, karate, or tai chi chuan. It should be understood that movement facility is not a means to an end; it is part of the way things get realized. A dancer's body and its capabilities are not his tool or his instrument. It is an intimate part of what he is and does, and who he is. The body is as basic as a stretch reflex propelling him into the air, as tender as his involuntarily softening to a touch, and as vital as the flood of memories and images coloring the mood and dynamics of his movement. There is no separation. Improvisors respond as an integrated whole, and improv must be pursued as such.

Part of this integrated whole is the performer's individual movement and response style. That style is usually stimulating, provocative, commanding, and appealing (even if in a quirky way). There is a richness and depth that becomes part of the improv. It is interesting to note that in India only mature dancers—those with life experiences—are allowed to improvise in performance.

For improv performers there is also the respect for the craft and art of improvisation: the readiness to engage the unknown, the cultivation of risk, the disciplined freedom of the moment, the galvanizing effect of an unfolding form.

There is also something else, hard to describe, possibly a result of the creative consciousness that we discuss in chapter 2, "Movement, the Foundation of Dance Improvisation." It is involvement, the kind that transforms the moment, creating a presence and whetting the audience's curiosity. The movement, infused with energy and particularity, becomes projected and invites our involvement. An audience provides the added edge and exhilaration.

How do you make the transition from the supportive atmosphere of the studio to a public performance? The invasion of the public eye into what is basically a private act can be an enormous step. In improv it includes not only an attitude change but a willingness to give up any sense of preciousness. (Obviously you would not have a performance with beginners, for besides terrifying them you would be defeating your own purposes. Even experienced movers who do exciting things in class don't always make the transition well, or care to.)

Improvising in front of an audience can be unsettling, and your usual responsive, spontaneous creativity can dry up like a mirage. Self-consciousness can suddenly yank you out of the driver's seat, especially when you sense the audience fidgeting, yawning, or looking for the nearest exit. You are on the spot. There is no chance to revise, cut, take a walk, or give up; you are in performance and must see it through for better or worse.

The biggest danger for improv in performance is that it can get b-o-r-i-n-g fast: it goes on and on ("I thought it ended ten minutes ago; why are they still up there?"); lacks a reason for being ("So what?"); or has no internal structure ("It doesn't go anywhere"). Even worse, it may become self-indulgent ("They look like they are having a good time, but spare me"). But even assuming experienced improvisers who are connected to the material, the problem is usually a lack of internal structuring.

One solution is to give some control to a non-improviser. There can be a leader (as in class) who adds options, changes directions, sanctions and encourages tangents. Less obviously, an accompanist or co-improviser could provide some focusing, encouraging a change or bringing it to an end. The first solution lends a workshop-demonstration orientation to the showing. The second relies on the musician or control improviser to have good forming skills, while maintaining an outside viewer's orientation. Whether or not someone acts as leader, the movers remain responsible for the internal form, focus, content, and overall direction of the piece.

Another solution is to set the end:

• You have only twenty sets of four beats.
• A warning alarm rings after three minutes and then you need to bring it to a close in one minute.
• Resolve as the music does.
• The improv continues but the curtain comes down.
• A stagehand carries off the dancer.

Even the most informal showing has a sense of theater, so the improviser who is interested in performance must be willing and able to mobilize quickly, come to the point, listen and find the form, and finally seek and risk the unknown. She must have the courage of her responses and the craft to develop them, the ability to stay honestly sensitive and connected while keeping her objective observer alive and functioning.

Only some groups or individuals are ready for or even interested in gearing themselves for performance. If you have such a group, wean them gradually away from the private and toward the public act of improvisation by building their performance skills. Have them perform for each other singly or in groups. Then discuss freely what worked and what didn't. Often they won't believe that the slow or still moments worked, even though they know it was right at the time. Point out what they may have missed or rejected because they were concerned about appearance. Use the progression of exercises that develop objectivity as presented in chapter 9, "Advanced Challenges."

After a while you can have an informal showing, for special friends, of a session in progress—with no promises or guaranteed results. You may want to start with improvs you have done before, the well-loved ones. The movers will not be bored with them because they invariably will not turn out the same (that, after all, is the one thing you can count on with improv). You can even add new options or restrictions, but at least the movers will be on familiar territory. When choosing an improv for performance (especially for a lay audience) it is best to use one with an easily discernible internal structure or one with clear roles and relationships. This will give both the audience and your inexperienced improv performers something to follow and hold on to.

The first time outsiders are present, getting started is the hardest part, so have the group warm up in their accustomed fashion. You can do this before people arrive, as they arrive, or as part of the presentation. Then go on to a couple of shorties with only a few options. For a while stay away from heavy personal images, for the sake of both the movers and the audience; they may choose that direction once they get going, but leave the decision to them. Even after a group has experience in front of an audience, start simply and gradually build in intensity and complexity.

With a more formal showing you may want to give a lecture demonstration where you introduce the audience to the nature of dance improvisation. Educating them about some of its goals and skills will help them understand it better and give them particular things to watch for. Emphasize that its beauty and challenge lie in its being ephemeral, spontaneous, and precarious.

Sometimes improv can serve one specific part of an otherwise set piece of choreography. Here it is advisable not to use dancers without improv experience. Of course you could use part of the rehearsal period to familiarize them with improvisation in general as well as the specific improv. But no sane choreographer would rely on unenthusiastic or un-improv-rehearsed dancers to carry off an improv section. (See the section for choreographers in chapter 12, "Specific Populations," for ways of incorporating improv into choreography.)

Some dance companies that would never dream of improvising in front of adults make their bread and butter improvising for children in schools. Here the pacing needs to be fast and the content varied; fantasy, intense drama, fun and exciting movement, slapstick, as well as highly charged issues are all appealing to this difficult but rewarding audience.

An audience can be requested to provide the stimulus for the improv—a word, phrase, or situation. They can be invited to join in the event, in which case the group members need to accept and interact with them generously, accommodating whatever leads they may spark. Sharing the stage is an act of communal significance, for it acknowledges the basic tenet that performance is an interactive event. Its roots in ritual reach far back and have unconscious, powerful connections which can well be capitalized upon. Whatever the structure, the audience does participate, if not with body or voice, then with attention: accelerating the risk, sharpening the edge, and supporting the performer's involvement with their own.[1]

[1]See Louise Steinman, *The Knowing Body: Elements of Contemporary Performance and Dance* (Boulder, Co.: Shambhala, 1986). "The Unexpected" is an excellent chapter dealing with improv in performance.

11 Special Situations

Ironically, improv's many options and freedoms create a double-edged sword. The opportunities it provides for expression can also allow for the indulgence of self and the exaggeration of idiosyncracies. This can become a behavioral problem that affects the learning and creative experience. It is your responsibility as leader to deal with that behavior in order to nurture a supportive environment for all present.

The first and most important thing to remember is to treat everyone with respect as an individual. Usually their behavioral problems have nothing to do with the class but are manifestations of chronic personality quirks or a temporary outside circumstance. You are not a therapist, but a facilitator of a smoothly functioning dance improv experience. Remember that the primary goal is to integrate these people into the group.

A behavioral problem feeds on itself and quickly grows worse if not confronted; don't let it drag on, hoping for the best. Often a problem can be dealt with by talking to the individual tactfully and in private, so try that first. Once they see themselves and their actions as others do they may spontaneously change their own behavior. Sometimes the problem is simply the result of a misconception. As in all learning, awareness is the first step; if they acknowledge the problem (although sometimes with elaborate justification) they have taken the first step and perhaps can then make a concerted effort to change. You can help by devising special rules for that individual ("Don't touch anyone until they touch you") while continuing to provide encouragement and positive reinforcement along the way.

Another thing to consider is that the person may already be well aware of his problem, having tried to solve it in the past. It may be a monkey on his back in other classes, at work, or socially. You can provide an opportunity to deal with it in a different mode. Since improv tends to induce some degree of reflection and work in selfimage, using a nonverbal experiential approach may just be the key that works.

Sometimes a movement experience is a good way to reinforce the verbal identification of the issue. After all, we should avail ourselves of the medium we are working in. Much can happen in movement. People have actually physically put others where they think they belong, or held their hands and almost force-fed them a more appropriate quality or energy level. Sometimes you can specifically ask other group members to help: have a secure, creative mover seek out the wallflower to move with.

At other times the solution is as simple as exposing them to a range of possible responses so they don't lock themselves in a corner. Or you can think up new improv structures that focus on the difficulty. Keep in mind the possibility of killing two birds with one stone when you are creating problem-solving improvisations. For example, a focus on small or minimal movement might be an exaggeration of one person's problems but a radical departure for someone else.

Despite these explanations, examples, and suggestions, there is only so much you can do. While it may be appropriate to take some class time to deal with individual problems (because one person's problem can become a class problem and a solution is in everyone's best interest), there is no reason why that issue should become the focus of the term. If you are concerned, you may want to seek advice from someone you respect and possibly even work individually with the person who is having trouble.

In the next several pages, we'll describe a few of the classic behavior problems and suggest ways of dealing with them. These are presented as stereotypes, offered this way partly for convenience and partly in comradeship. There should be some comfort in knowing that other leaders have encountered and dealt with similar situations. But since people do not come in stereotyped packages, you will need to modify your approach to meet the specifics of each situation. Our suggested solutions are merely a place for you to take off from. In the final analysis, the best thing to do is what feels right to you.

The Space Glutton

Somehow, during his years of upbringing and acculturation, this person has acquired a sense of private space that disregards our societal norms and taboos. He is probably a big mover as well as being the "touchy-feely" type, and so on two counts manages to invade and annoy. Such behavior is disruptive; it offends individuals and directly affects the group's progress. Because it encroaches on others this particular problem cannot be ignored. Try the following improv.

Poison
The movers run in, out, and through each other without touching (everyone else is "poison"). Initially, the whole room is available, but the space is gradually limited to half, then a quarter, then an eighth, or a corner. At this point a signal allows everyone to burst out into the big open space for a few lush moments before immediately returning to the confines of the tiny space.

Repetition of the burst/return pattern several times addresses simultaneously the issues of space confinement and nontouching.

Other improvs that address this problem are those based on personal kinesphere—try them individually at first and then in pairs, emphasizing that each person should pay careful attention to the reaction of his partner.

The Dictator

There are certain individuals who dominate the group to such a degree that it is uncomfortable for everyone. They impose themselves, their style, ideas, and preferences on the others without realizing it or intending to. We are not speaking about the more common extroverts whom everyone thoroughly enjoys and respects, but of a rather more intense and perhaps less self-aware personality. Their insensitivity can be due to an overblown reaction to an inner lack of self-confidence, or a myriad of other psychological causes. Regardless, the symptoms are clear, and the results are disturbing to the group.

• Talk to her.
• Use improvs such as **Mirroring** which utilize a leader/follower format, switching roles according to your directions rather than at the discretion of the movers.
• Privately give her instructions that emphasize response, asking

her to follow those for a specific improv during the next session. Afterward, have her write down the differences she noticed in how other people treated her and how she felt in the situation.

The Wallflower

At the other end of the spectrum are the people who don't get involved at all. They do little and say even less. They look around, sometimes watching what everyone else is doing as though hungering for a clue that they can pick up on and use themselves. Sometimes they even nod in understanding at all of your directions, yet do not change or respond. Because they seem to have little to offer, others tend to avoid them when it comes time to pair off, thus making the situation worse. Often they want to sit out and watch; once is fine, but it should not be allowed to become habitual.

This behavior may be an expression of low self-confidence, fear, or apathy. Whatever its underlying causes, such people will obviously get limited if any benefit from the class if they remain passive or timid. If you can get them involved, they may blossom.

• In a paired structure, have your most enthusiastic yet patient student partner him. Perhaps some of that excitement will spark a response.

• Do improvs that require isolated and/or limited movement of small body parts which then develop to large movements, more body parts, and spatial locomotion.

• Begin with visualization and ask that the process going on in the mind's eye gradually be made visible in one tiny part of the body, then another, and another until you get the whole body moving.

The Dancer

Here is the person who has had some ballet, jazz, or acrobatic training, but little or no modern dance, and no improvisation. His only movement response derives from a specific technical vocabulary: arabesques, classical poses, jazzy combinations, or segments from dance routines. He is not showing off, but trying to use what he already knows about movement—quite a natural response.

• Explain that you are seeking fresh movement and put a taboo on

any known vocabulary: "In this improv you may only do movement that you have *never* done before."
• If he has ballet training, emphasize angular and asymmetrical body positions and movement; stress flowing and curved ones if his background is jazz-oriented.
• Use themes that inherently demand movement that is weighted, passive, or heavy, or that requires moving on the ground using postures of sitting, lying, dragging, crawling, and rolling.
• Set an improv which begins with a movement common in that person's vocabulary and inch by inch move it a step away. For example, an arabesque: "Make one part droopy . . . another . . . another. Start again with a clean ballet arabesque and this time let it twist and droop. Play with a variety of droopy and twisted arabesques, exaggerating the weighted quality while making it lower and lower; let it become heavier and crumble."

THE PERFORMER

With this person every movement is a performance, a look-at-me opportunity. She may be overly conscious of the mirror, checking out every movement; or she may repeatedly position herself close to you or clearly in your immediate line of vision to make sure you're watching. If observers are present or part of the group is watching, she will usually take front and center. The difficulty is that although she goes through the motions, the creative spark is never lit. That is because her work is oriented outward rather than motivated from within. The emphasis needs to be shifted from what the experience looks like to what the experience feels like.
• Remind her to work with eyes closed.
• Have the group face away from the mirror.
• Do improvs focused on the tactile and the audible rather than on visual designs.
• Work in ways that are quiet, small, or minimal, thus reducing or nullifying any show-off value.

THE ODDBALL

Every so often there is one member of the class whom everyone else finds offensive. He may be considered weird or creepy, be unkempt or have body odor, be finicky, boisterous, or extremely dramatic. Often his movements are odd, and that becomes yet another reason why no one wants to work with him. Yet it is evident that this person is sincerely involved and does contribute (sometimes too much). Although he may be extremely bright, with a complex mind and intellect, he probably has no idea that he is considered strange or undesirable by others. The Oddball, it must be realized, can have a lot to offer because of, rather than in spite of, his idiosyncracy.

• When partnering activities occur, be aware of pairing him with all others in the class, not just the submissive few who lack the initiative to resist his presence or intrusion. This is not only democratic: he may find someone who is able to relate to and appreciate him, and an important liaison may be found.

• Do an improv about strange style or weird movement, noticing what types of things he considers strange. See what insights can be gained in the discussion following the improv concerning subjective and objective feelings about strangeness.

• Use a follow-the-leader technique so the people in the class have an opportunity to do what is natural to them and in turn are encouraged to try the different movement styles of others.

• If the problem is body odor, deal with it directly and privately.

The Intense One

Very occasionally you will find someone who gets so intense that it frightens others. The intensity might be bodily (in which case it can be physically threatening) or emotional (which could have either physical or psychological repercussions). This person has to be confronted. It is fine that he is involved but the danger posed to others is real and must be acknowledged.

When told he is too intense, he may say, "Oh no, I was just fooling around. I wasn't really going off the deep end." This type has the ability to let movement pour out with no censor, while sufficiently disassociating himself from it to maintain a rational distance. A caution to the mover, plus perhaps bringing it up before the group simply and directly can often allay fears, clear the air, and cause a change. Sometimes he needs to be warned about hurting himself as he wham-bams around. Ask him to control the energy, not stop it; to funnel it, thus using it to advantage. You may even positively point out that great art has strong intensity but is focused.

- Do an improv about passivity, about being "laid back," easygoing.
- Since intensity usually goes hand-in-hand with large activity, work with small movements, small spaces, and attention to detail.
- Do an improv on caring for others and building interpersonal trust.
- Try to have him use his energy in a very focused and directed way. Or, go in the other direction: try to get a breakthrough by using his undirected intensity for all its worth, making it the fulcrum of an improv experience and pushing it even beyond his limits. Afterward talk about it in class or in private; the discussion could be insightful for both of you.

12 Specific Populations

As leaders of improv we sometimes find opportunities to work with populations other than the ones we are accustomed to. Can we get a third grade class to improvise? What would we do with a group of people in wheelchairs? Should we try? Though we are specialists in dance improv, do we know enough about these people to make our knowledge beneficial to them in their particular situations? Will we be useless or, even worse, harmful? What can we do that will interest them and how can we present it in an appropriate way?

Before we consider these questions it should be stressed that the material presented so far in this book is basic to all populations. Space, phrasing, gravity, and so forth, are inherent in every movement experience. The same issues of format, leadership, pragmatics, content, and personality types, while colored by circumstances, are applicable in every situation. The difference in the point of departure for the various groups becomes evident once their specific nature is identified and understood.

While we do not attempt to treat any population in depth, we offer some suggestions for successfully adapting movement improvisation to such diverse groups as choreography students, actors, children, people with disabilities. You should begin by asking yourself the following critical question: "Am I, as leader in this setting, willing and able to make the necessary adjustments in the methods I use and in my expectations?" The answer calls for more than altruism; it demands that you honestly assess your own skills, prejudices, and interests. Only then can you determine whether working with any given group of people will be mutually beneficial. (Of course, sometimes your attitudes and abilities will not become evident until you've begun work and are in the midst of the situation.)

If you decide to go ahead, the material in this chapter should help you with some of the "hows." We also suggest some books which address the specific populations. It is a good idea to familiarize yourself with the group and give yourself some background from specialists in the field, before jumping in on the basis of enthusiasm, good intention, and general knowledge. We conclude this chapter with a short look at dance therapy.

We have decided to use a single improvisational structure, based on the idea of a journey, and adapt it to the specific needs and goals of most of the populations. It is not the first improv to be given to each group but is rather an illustration of how instructions can reflect the concerns of the specific population. The following is a neutral, skeletal framework for the journey improv. (In instances where no detailed variation of it is given you may want to develop one of your own.[1])

Journey
You are going on a journey. Find a place to start. Let a pulsing begin to move you. It radiates, spreading to other parts of your body. It starts to move you through space. Something gets in your way; how can you get past it? You are almost at the end of your journey. Go the last little way and bring it to an end.

Of the many ways there are to use improv with each population we will suggest a few, with the implicit understanding that these are less than the tip of the iceberg. It is up to you to identify further goals and decide how to reach them. The following four objectives may help you plan.

• *Pleasure*: the simple satisfaction that results from self-initiated movements; the joy of movement for its own sake; playful experimentation in an explorative, expressive, nonjudgmental setting; interacting and sharing with others; being creative and having that creativity honored and respected.

• *Physical well-being*: greater suppleness and better coordination; new movement skills; increased cardiovascular strength, muscular range, coordination, and endurance; increased sensual and kin-

[1]In chapter 8, "Create Your Own Improv," there are a number of developments of this same structure. You may want to look at these for a more neutral, less specific set of instructions.

esthetic sensitivity; the chemical, physiological high of exuberant exercise.

• *Psychological enrichment:* raising, addressing, and solving issues of body-image and self-image; dealing with inner turmoils and problems; working on relationships and other therapy-related issues.

• *Conceptual growth:* increased understanding of dance as an art form including such aspects as abstraction, form, and style; exploration of aesthetic concepts; a deeper understanding of people, their behaviors and motives.

Obviously these categories are not exclusive; they mix naturally, feeding each other. For example, when working with children's creative movement, the primary objectives may be among those identified as pleasure, yet the activity automatically cultivates physical skills and produces conceptual or psychological gains as well. A perceptive and well-informed leader will keep these cross-fertilizations and fringe benefits in mind and be ever ready to further them.

Now let's look at some of the many situations where dance improv can be and has been used successfully.

CHOREOGRAPHERS

Improvisation is often used in teaching choreography. Since students of choreography are constantly on the hunt for movement, any improv can be considered field work. But it is also a good way to experience the choreographic concepts before actually applying them in composition.[2] For example, choreographers are interested in form as well as content. Learning to see and identify the variety of natural structures and substructures which intuitively emerge during an improv helps sharpen their understanding of form and subsequently the ability to create it in a dance.

If you are helping beginning choreographers to find new movement during an improv you may occasionally point out a particular movement so they can focus on it. "That turn-fall; try it again. Where does it want to go?" This identification brings the kinesthetic experience to a conscious level. It conveys to them a sense of the move-

---

[2]This approach to learning choreography is the basis of our book *The Intimate Act of Choreography* (Pittsburgh: University of Pittsburgh Press, 1982).

ment's integrity and power and the mover's capacity to create. It also points up the need to develop their own observer in order to capitalize on intuitive resources. (However, do not make the mistake of taking over the process of forming and selecting too frequently; they must learn to make their own decisions.) They need to be able to identify, extract, and remember those things that worked well so later when composing they can make the more objective editorial choices about its appropriateness and placement in the piece. Of course, the more advanced choreographers are clearer about what to keep and what to discard. The exercises in chapter 9, "Advanced Challenges," which help build objectivity are particularly useful in this regard.

Journey (for choreographers)
Begin by trying several shapes. Hold each one for a few moments. Choose the most interesting in terms of design and/or intent and let this be how your journey begins. Feel where the tensions are and let the movement start there, radiating out, maybe gradually, maybe in spurts, spreading to other parts. Notice what is happening; stay with it; clarify it. Repeat any tidbit that works particularly well. Feel it as a phrase. Good. Do the phrase again this time letting it continue to build and move you out into space. Are you heading toward a specific spot with focused clarity, or meandering and unsure of your destination? Choose and develop one of these. Something gets in your way. What are you going to do? Develop it. Cull the important parts. Try them, emphasizing their distinctive aspects: is it the building, driving momentum of the rhythm, or the funny slip-sliding step and the tossing of your head and fingers? Elaborate and refine. This time finish the encounter and go toward the end of your journey. How does it end? Is it different from where and how you began? If so, emphasize this difference. If not, how is it similar? Will the ending movement fade out, rise to an exclamatory end, or continue as the lights fade?

Discussion and follow-up: Describe the overall form of the improv. What were the high points? Close your eyes and picture yourself doing one of the movement sequences. Now show us that one. In composing a dance on this theme, what would you keep? How would you improve on that? What else is needed?

Create your own improv to help you explore that and/or to fill in the gaps that still exist. Improvise. Recapture and refine. What is the form now? Can you draw it? Be very clear about the different subsections. Choreograph a dance, "The Journey."

In addition to functioning as a resource pool of new movement and/or thematic content for a piece, improv can also be used as one element within set choreography.

• One or more dancers have set movements; one or more improvise.

• A duet is basically set but is performed with a slightly different edge each night: dancer A refuses eye contact while dancer B touches dancer A every so often; both eliminate the use of the arms; dancer B sinks and turns away whenever possible.

• Five specific movements are given; vary the order, timing, facing, repetition, and so on, for each performance.

For additional ideas on using improv in choreography, see chapter 9, "Advanced Challenges," and chapter 10, "In Performance."

Dance Educators

What about using improv to teach some of the academic aspects of movement? Although dance educators have a strong appreciation of the value of the experiential, we sometimes fall into the academic trap of separating head learning from body learning within certain areas of our own discipline. The teacher of dance theory and criticism, movement analysis, music for dancers, dance ethnology, and dance history could all benefit from an occasional use of improv.

For example, in a dance ethnology class it is all very well to know the names and contents of dances, learn about their forerunners, the concurrent social and political institutions, and so on, but to move with a sense of the style (in an improvisatory setting) allows an experiential entry into an otherwise foreign form. The idea, of course, would not be to get the individual dance or specific steps to occur spontaneously; the recreation of Bugaku or of a Yanomamo Indian dance requires the precision of notators and reconstruction-ists. The goal is rather to impart experientially an appreciation of the culture and the values it inculcates. Incorporate in the improv what is striking about the culture, especially when it is significantly different from our experience; for example, in certain castes in India women must keep their eyes downcast when men are around. For material for the improv look to details of social status or behavioral roles, of attitudes toward the environment, or work habits and patterns, customs, rites, physical attributes, dance rhythms, and especially the music. The improvisational setting provides an opportunity for the participants to identify and reify the values of the culture while giving them an opportunity to find their own ways of physically interpreting those values. The movement emerges from the given philosophy or set of priorities. It brings the foreign or exotic within reach and gives the students a personal, experiential reference point from which to perceive and understand it. (See **Other Cultures.**)

CHILDREN

Working with children has an intensity about it that is unlike working with any other group. Consider children's unique characteristics when designing and guiding their creative movement experience.

• *Love of movement.* Work with pure movement concepts as subject matter.

• *Short attention span.* Use improvs which have lots of alternatives and tangents; also have a bevy of shorter, pointed improvs that share a common focus, allowing you to proceed from one to another quickly while maintaining unity and a primary objective.

• *High energy.* Use movement instructions, images, and ideas that suggest vigorous movement; alternate these with periods of quiet, and introspective work.

• *Importance of personal experience.* Connect improvs with subjects of immediate interest to them such as movement itself, popular films, holidays, a school project, current events, TV and cartoon heroes, pets, and sports.

• *Enlarged sense of the real and the fantastic.* Capitalize on themes of fantasy, science fiction, fairy tales, the supernatural, the surrealistic, and the superpowerful.

• *Need for quickly achieved gratification, recognition, and sense of accomplishment.* Repeatedly interject supportive comments on the work being done, both in process and immediately thereafter in the discussion.

• *Less adherence to social taboos or restrictions.* Investigate such areas as touch, facial expression, a wide range of vocal sounds, and the use of the weird or monstrous.

• *More direct connections between emotions and expression.* Awareness of this can suggest certain topics (highly animated or dramatic themes) and caution you against others which may have potent negative connotations or repercussions (scary material could lead to nightmares).

You can see from this list that characteristics often considered difficulties or challenges can work to your advantage, and theirs.

Journey (for children)

You're going on a trip. Find a place to start, get into a beginning shape and close your eyes. Where are you? Is it warm and fuzzy there, or slimy, or scratchy? Show me how the place feels. Something starts to move. Where is it? inside you? on the floor? in the air? Is it alive? It's moving onto your shoulder, oops, over to your belly. What's that like? Does it tickle, squeak, dart, squirm? How can you move the little feller around without using your hands? Let him into little places, your ear, under your arms. Now he's taking you into space. He could drag, fling, push, carry you where he wants to go. Use high spaces and low ones, let him move you backward or sideways as he takes you somewhere new. What's this new place like? Uh oh, suddenly something's gotten in your way— maybe a cobweb, or an extraterrestrial creature, maybe a hole, an animal, or a fire. How big is it? Is it moving and if so, how? How can you get past it—under, around, over, through? Maybe you will even want to take it home with you. Could you do that? Show me. Now you are home. Make it nice to be there for a while, and then finally cuddle down to sleep and dream about the adventure you just had.

There will be no shortage of input when it comes time to talking about this improv. All that you need ask is: "Who'd like to tell about how his journey started? Who was the creature who went with you?

How did he make you move? What got in the way? How'd you get by it?"

Another possibility is a journey based on different kinds of movement instead of on narrative or dramatic imagery.

Movement Journey (for children)

You're going to go through an obstacle course or a maze. You must follow the rules. First of all, travel a great distance low to the floor. Now worm your way out and up a wall until you are in a large open space.... As soon as you are free you become very heavy but you still need to travel.... Becoming less and less heavy you continue on, coming to blockages, quick turnabouts, skinny places, halls of jittering floors or rubbery walls....

Spontaneous creative movement and children go well together. All you need is love for them both, patience, and lots of energy.[3]

ACTORS

Actors respond enthusiastically to dance improv because they appreciate the expressive and communicative value of the body in movement and the value of the creative process. Furthermore, they are unusually receptive to trying out new things and pushing limits. For actors, movement improvisation is not an end in itself but a necessary tool for exploring and expanding their skills.

Dance improv can be used to widen the actor's range of movement and to define his personal movement style (his movement affinities, body image, and mannerisms). It gives him the freedom to take physical and emotional risks in his movement responses and to make them larger than life (this is especially useful when working with stylized plays). It also brings him an understanding of the various aspects of space, time, and energy: how they influence the quality of movement and how, in turn, that influences the interpretation of the

[3]Suggested reading: Mary Joyce, *First Steps in Teaching Creative Dance to Children* (Palo Alto, Cal.: Mayfield, 1980), and the great variety of books by Barbara Mettler.

nonverbal aspects of his portrayals. Through dance improv he can refine his characterization.

Improv also provides opportunities to explore physically certain pivotal issues in the character's hidden agenda. At any given moment in a play, the character's purpose plays a major part in determining how the actor portrays the role. The obstacle section of the journey improv provides a setting in which the actor pays particular attention to exploring his character's internal attitudes toward an outwardly stated objective. In particular, the way he deals with the obstacle in light of his resolve furnishes insight into his drives and motives which may be only implicit in the text.

Journey (for actors)

Preparation: Choose some character you're working on or interested in. Conduct the entire improv as that character. Give yourself a few quiet moments to let the character enter your body, thinking, feeling. Select something significant from your character's makeup or past. As you focus on that feel it affecting you.

Now begin walking around the room. Try a wide and stable stride, then one that's turned in. Which is more appropriate? Continue with that while trying different speeds, keeping your significant feature in mind. Try placing the center of weight up in the chest, then down low in the pelvis; choose which feels right. Try walking straight, or in meandering paths. Which one is right? Try focusing inward or out. If out, are you zeroing in on something specific or are you all inclusive, taking in everything? Is that from curiosity? from cool, detached observation? from fear? Recall something your character is particularly proud of—where in the body might that reside? Allow that part to lead you into the space. Is there anything you're ashamed of that you want to hide or minimize, or something that holds you back? Where is it located? How does it physically impede or limit your movement—exaggerate that. Allow the various constituents of the movement to clarify and jell: the timing, spatial aspects, energy. Sink into your character's postures and movements...become that person.

Now identify something which you (as your character) need or want to get to. It may be geographical, a state of being, status, person, or any other objective. What is your attitude toward it? Are you anxious to get there? nervous? eager? What are you passing through along the way—serene areas or chaotic ones, full of obstacles or smooth and easy, filled with dangerous unknowns or engaging surprises? Does it annoy or delight you, impede your progress or aid it? Do you loiter? Remember to keep your character's primary objective in mind. At some point, encounter an obstacle of some sort, in the terrain or in the form of another character, symbol, animal, invisible blockage, rainbow, parade, idea, or problem. If it's intangible, give it a physical reality, a shape, texture, size, energy. How does it affect you? Notice changes, if any, in your own movement or tension. How will you deal with the obstacle? If you don't get past it, how will you resolve the action? If you do, continue on the last leg of the journey toward your initial objective.

Note if and how that objective has changed. Is your anxiety increasing as you make your final approach, or are you rushing toward it? When you finally arrive bring it to an end (which may or may not be peaceful).

Discussion: Who was your character? Identify bodily details of how you moved. What specific physical identifications did you make which you can keep and use? Did that physicality remain constant throughout the journey, and if not, how and when did it change and what does that tell you about your character? What can you learn from your character's attitude toward the objective? Was the goal one that is explicit or implicit within the parameters of the play? What was the obstacle and how did you deal with it? Did you make any concessions or self-transformations along the way? What? How? Why?

Used in this way, the journey improv becomes a vehicle for working on character development by way of strategically guided options discovered, chosen, and developed in movement improv.[4]

[4]Suggested reading: Constantin Stanislavski, *The Actor Prepares* (New York: Theatre Arts, 1948), and *Building a Character* (New York: Theatre Arts, 1977); Peter Brook, *The Empty Space* (New York: Atheneum, 1978); and Viola Spolin, *Improvisation for the Theater: A Handbook of Teaching and Directing Techniques* (Evanston, Ill.: Northwestern University Press, 1983).

SENIOR CITIZENS

We are speaking here of people for whom the simple passage of years has made their bodies wear down, creak more, and run slower or less smoothly than well-oiled new ones. Of course, there may often be associated problems as well, such as loss of short-term memory, loneliness, paranoia, and frustration over their diminishing physical and mental capacities.

Within the physical limitations of their age group, they can move, explore, and relate. The joy of creating a movement or rhythmic pattern, sharing it with others, and erupting spontaneously into unified, communal participation and engagement is hardly lessened one iota because it is not a huge jumping or locomotor pattern that takes them charging across the floor.

It is said that the heart never grows old, nor the feelings within. Use this adage like a potion to help generate responses. For instance, when you play music, particularly music that was well known and loved in their youth, older people will be internally motivated to move as they did in former years, for muscle memory lasts a lifetime. The movement may be in the form of swaying or clapping; in some cases it may take a more active or larger form, as they join hands, waltz a few steps, or spontaneously dish up a few counts of a jig. If the group is sedentary, let them be expressive with their upper bodies, their arms, heads, hands; encourage them to wave their canes or keep the tempo with the tapping of a foot.

Remember that their experiential bank is rich; they have traveled a long way. They have vast storehouses of memories, events, and cultural traditions to draw upon from a lifetime of living. Take them on a journey back through a town of their youth, into a time with their parents, a vacation, a special outing or a moment with a loved one; let them choose the street to stroll down, the things that happen on the way. With this orientation toward the journey improv, you are literally affording them an opportunity to relive cherished moments from their past.

It has been established that such reminiscing can play an important role in lowering depressive affect, increasing self-esteem and socialization, and encouraging cognitive reorganization in people whose age has caused confusion or disorientation. The elderly actually function better as they recall and relive their younger selves. Movement improvisation which capitalizes on reminiscence offers them a way to progress from the sensory experience to a cognitive, emotional and/or symbolic one.

As with any group, the benefits of movement are apparent: increased cardiovascular and muscular activity, realistic body image, and enhancement of remaining mobility skills. A ninety-two-year-old woman said that she wouldn't allow anyone to pick up the newspaper from her front porch and bring it in for her because, "If I stopped doing that today, I wouldn't be able to do it tomorrow." It is instructive for us to really hear everything that her statement conveys: the need for continued movement, the relationship of physical capacity to psychological and actual independence, the continued significance of body image (regardless of age), not to mention (but not to forget) the necessary redefinition of physical activity and exertion.

Certainly exploration of the elements of movement, form, and abstraction would be rewarding. For while the movement range of the elderly is limited in many cases, their appreciation of aesthetics is not. Many have more time to read and to attend art exhibits, theater, and dance concerts.

The elderly also have an interest in psychological explorations of current concerns. For many of them, a major issue is that they are reaching the end of their current journey of life. Either they have a keen and valid interest in death or a fear of it and—popular opinion notwithstanding—many of them would rather face than avoid that concern. They may even see death as a new journey.

It is not the quantity but the quality of the movement (its kinetic, emotional, and cognitive significance) which makes it a wise and worthy investment for the elderly.[5]

People with Disabilities

Included in this group are people with a wide range of impairments, either physical or mental, and at times, both. The visually impaired,

[5]Suggested reading: Liz Lerman, *Teaching Dance to Senior Adults* (Springfield, Ill.: C. C. Thomas, 1984).

the hearing impaired, slow learners, and the orthopedically impaired fall into this category. While there are a variety of conditions which impose restrictions, an improv leader can work quite successfully so long as she remembers the population's limitations and abilities.

The issue to resolve is whether or not movement improvisation is practical with the population you are considering working with. The critical factors are (1) whether or not they are capable of sufficient movement, and (2) the level at which they can understand and follow instructions.

Clearly, additional training in psychology and physical therapy is needed to work with some groups, and this is best left to specialists. But many people with disabilities are approachable by a dance improv specialist who can apply commonsense guidelines. Movement leaders who work in institutional settings have the advantage of consulting attending therapists and doctors. Leaders not so fortunate in having access to such specialists would be well advised to seek them out for consultation if situations so warrant.

When you are setting up the group make it clear that it is a class in dance improvisation and not a physical therapy or a dance therapy group. For some people, an initial disability causes a chain reaction. For example, a physical impairment can generate psychological problems, which in turn can cause perceptual losses or disturbances, which may result in cognitive distortions or failures. If therapy-related issues do come up in the course of the work, as well they might, deal with them in a sensible, cool-headed, and compassionate way. If problems requiring professional therapeutic help are identified, talk privately to the participant, possibly referring them to a registered dance therapist or physical therapist.

The nature of the impairment will determine the limitations placed on movement responses, the types of cues employed for giving instructions, and the mode of presentation of the improv material. You will have to evaluate the problems of each particular population in order to choose your approach. Here are a few basic questions to consider.

• What sensory or movement capacity is missing or limited? Is it a new or long-term disability?

• What other channels of communication (sensory modes) and/or areas of movement exist? Consider these from both their receptive and expressive aspects.

• How can you adapt instructions, format, and content?

• What might be some general fears or reservations with regard to themes, movement in general, and dance improvisation in particular?

Once working with a group, if you have practical questions about procedure, limitations, or what would make things more accessible for them, the best way of finding out is by asking them directly.

The Visually Impaired

While some people with sensory disabilities automatically compensate by developing the remaining senses, others do not. Thus improvs that stress the kinetic and tactile can be especially helpful for the visually impaired. For example, a good improv is a duet where one person uses different parts of her body to mold the shape of the other. (For more improv ideas, see chapter 14, "Sources," especially those in the categories Self to Inner Self, Self to Outer Self; and in units 3 and 4, Sensory Awakening and Elements of Movement.)

In general, make commonsense preparations. Begin by orienting the group to the physical surroundings (asking them the best way to do so). For individual work, make sure each person has lots of space. For pair work, allow the partners to make touch identification at the outset, so they are clear as to whom they are working with and where that person is. The better lit you can get the room, the more those with partial sight will be able to see. Remember, never assume that all members of the group are totally blind or that everyone has been completely blind from birth. The category *visually impaired* ranges from the totally blind to the partially sighted, and many have lost sight through accident or illness.

In giving instructions it is unnecessary to omit visual imagery and references. Words such as "see" and "find" are a natural part of the language, and have expressional value that functions quite apart from their literal meaning. Their omission only draws attention to the impairment. (In the same way, don't drop movement words and expressions—jump for joy, dragging your heels—with people who are orthopedically impaired, nor aural words—hear, listen, sounds—with the hearing impaired.) The best rule is to use expressions naturally.

Nevertheless, since sight is not the main mode of perception for the visually impaired, a sensible adaptation would be some shift in emphasis from visual cues or images to ones that are kinesthetic, aural, tactile, or even olfactory. You will want to experiment, providing instructions and props which stimulate these senses.

After getting to know the group you could develop a journey improv from the undifferentiated one given at the beginning of the chapter. One possibility would be to have the journey occur in one place using the limbs and torso for exploration. Traveling may be the goal of a second journey after they've gained a measure of familiarity with the room, the structure and content of the improv in a stationary version, and with movement improv in general. Try having them travel along a rope strung across the room. Tie ribbons on the rope near where it ends.

The Hearing Impaired

The hearing impaired, by the very nature of their disability, already make extensive use of the two primary aspects of dance—the kinetic and the visual. Their language, signing, depends on both. Sign language is physical, expressive, and already has a rich history in non-verbal forms. Some signs have a variety of meanings that become explicit with the use of accompanying facial expressions, gestures, or postures. This group's familiarity with movement and sight as their primary communicative links generally eases their access to movement improvisation.

A main consideration when working with the hearing impaired is the format of the presentation. Once they begin moving, they will often be unable to see you. Whether you sign yourself or have an interpreter doing it for you, the continuous feed-in format is not suitable. However, this does not preclude giving timing clues along the way. For example, you could outline the general structure of the improv in a concise set of instructions given before any movement begins (possibly using the basic journey improv at the beginning of this chapter). But also at that time, you could agree upon a few signals to initiate specific occurrences. Turning out the lights could indicate the beginning of the internal pulse; a double flashing—off/

on, off/on—could signal the appearance of the obstacle; a touch on the shoulder could tell them to approach the end of their journey. As you work with them over a period of time, you will get to know which cues and formats work best. During the discussions, ask for ways to improve your presentation.

Remember that, as with the visually impaired, any group will likely include various degrees of impairment, so do not categorically exclude all auditory stimuli or vocal responses. In fact, the hearing impaired particularly enjoy strong rhythmic music because they can feel the powerful base rhythms via vibrations in the floor. You will need to work with decibel levels considerably higher than you are used to or comfortable with, but it is well worth it. Just as for hearing people, pulse and repetition provide an organic connection to the natural rhythm cycles of life.

As a movement specialist you will no doubt become fascinated by their language and you may want to learn to sign (if you don't already) so you can interact and communicate more directly.

Slow Learners

Slow learners (the mentally retarded) benefit from the physical and creative aspects of improvisation, especially in achieving a wonderful sense of accomplishment and pride. The enormously successful work of the Special Olympics can serve as a useful model for movement improvisation with this population. Some basic guidelines are:
- Keep the tasks and the instructions simple.
- Repeat the instructions often to encourage concentration and insure comprehension.
- Work in groups with a high leader-to-mover ratio.
- Reward any involvement, initiative, or response with positive, overly repetitive support and encouragement.
- Give each participating individual something—a name tag, a ribbon—which identifies him as a member/achiever of that activity.

The improv structure should be simple; don't offer too many alternatives. The training of slow learners emphasizes both mutual support within the group and independent responsibility, so their journey improv might focus on helping an imaginary creature (a pet or a friend) get from place A, which is dull or gray (perhaps a dreary day or a lonely time), to place B, which is exciting and fun (say, a fireworks display or a party with lots of friends and music). Or the journey could be in the form of a trip to some place of special interest, such as a zoo or circus, where the emphasis can be on the variety of movement found there.

The primary objectives in working with this group are pleasure, physical well-being, and psychological enrichment (developing ego strength, coping with personal fears and depression, and so forth). Practice in independent problem-solving and the self-identifiable achievement of simple tasks, however imitative they may be, are also significant aids in their development.

In working with any disabled population, remember that the basic yardsticks of improvisation still pertain: personal involvement; discovery about the self, the self in relation to others, and the surrounding world; exploration of movement range, qualitative as well as quantitative; honesty of response; social interaction. These apply to everyone. A person who cannot see, hear, or do somersaults is still a human being with hopes and hates, a sense of humor, and emotional needs. Such people may also scheme and undermine, have hidden agendas, and arrive with lots of baggage, as we all do. But they take pride in accomplishment and derive pleasure from the act of communication and expression. Unfortunately, they are often credited with less than they are actually capable of. They enjoy being challenged; and the feeling of achievement that comes from mastering a difficult skill, or solving an enigmatic problem, will lift their spirits and be inherently rewarding.

THERAPY

Often without any intent on the part of the leader or mover, an improv session is therapeutic. The person feels better because he expressed pent-up anger, had an insight into a relationship, or connected two previously disconnected ideas or situations of personal significance. Often his behavior or attitude will change because of these insights. This is an appealing side benefit for many groups primarily intent on other goals. And while therapeutic ends can be fostered by an experienced leader, you must resist the temptation to take on the role of psychologist. Letting people talk about their feelings or express them physically is one thing; imposing an interpretation or forcing confrontations is another. Playing psychologist is irresponsible. You need extensive professional training to deal with problems that may surface; you *can* do harm. We present this section to give an idea of the field of dance therapy and the role dance improv plays within it.

Dance therapy, which unifies the discipline and knowledge of movement with that of psychology, began with people who were working in dance and creative movement who then moved more and more toward the area of psychology. It is now a separate field, taught in graduate schools and requiring certification which incorporates extensive theoretical knowledge and intensive guided work in the field.[6]

One of the underlying premises of dance therapy is that the state of mind—feelings, attitudes, perceptions, cognition—is directly influenced by the ways and means (posture, movement) of the body. Physical changes, therefore, can bring about mental changes. Moreover, given the emphasis on the verbal/conceptual in our society, the acknowledgment and use of movement as felt-thought is a step toward healing the split between the mind and the body.

In its brochure, the American Dance Therapy Association distinguishes dance/movement therapy "from other utilizations of dance which may be recreational or educational in nature by its focus on the nonverbal aspects of behavior and its use of movement as the process for intervention. Expressive and communicative behaviors are considered in treatment, with the express goal of integrating these behaviors with psychological aspects of the person."

Therapists work with movement in a number of different ways, of which dance improvisation is only one, albeit a main one. They analyze movement, postural patterns and restrictions, and prescribe guided movement experiences. They investigate areas of resistance, uncertainties, and underlying motivations for behavior which is undesirable from the client's (or society's) point of view. Sometimes dance therapists will work in conjunction with psychotherapists in a

[6]The American Dance Therapy Association (2000 Century Plaza, Suite 108, Columbia, Md., 21044) is an organization overseeing certification in this field. Some pre-therapy programs are available for undergraduates, but course work is generally at the graduate level.

format where the client pursues at length, with the psychotherapists, the insights and questions that come up during the movement session. The therapeutic population ranges from institutionalized patients to the "worried well"—the normal neurotic man or woman on the street. The specific case history guides the kind of therapy, as well as the content and nature of the improvisations chosen for use.

When working with the psychotic, the severely anxious, and people with character disorders, extensive individualized and in-depth work is needed and progress is slow. Conversely, the success one can expect when working with a *mildly* neurotic population is often greater and more rapid. For some people the tensions and complexities of daily life are at times hard to deal with alone. Some cultures have ways to support natural but difficult transitions as well as unexpected events. They deal with these in sophisticated and socially acceptable, noncognitive ways, such as wakes to mourn the dead, duels to satisfy personal honor, or the *I Ching* to aid in decision making. In certain areas of India where female behavior is strictly limited, it is acceptable for women to become possessed and dance wildly during the spring festival of Holi; this outburst of impassioned, improvised dance is a social safety valve. Our culture has lost most of these, a condition partially engendered by a leftover Puritan ethic that essentially denies the presence or expression of such drives as sex or aggression, upholds stoicism as a virtue, and clings to rational cognitive logic. (The many telephone "hot lines" primarily address an immediate crisis and do not deal with underlying causes.) Improvisation, when used in dance therapy, can address these needs and problems.

• It provides a forum for expression of pent-up emotions and a physical release of tension in a constructive and acceptable form.
• It allows one to deal with the total felt-sense of the problem.
• It lets individuals examine personal concerns through symbolic gestures or movement patterns:

After a while, the leader of a simple improv structure focusing on in-out movement asks the doer to choose one of the two and give it an identity. (The client thus personalizes from an abstract action to a specific element in her life.) The chosen movement, in or out, is then developed thematically according to its identity and the mover's attitude to it.

• It builds positive self-image: a strong and realistic body-image; a feeling of accomplishment in expanding one's range of movement; confidence in relating; and pride in being flexible in both leading and following and in group work.
• It provides ways to discover and try out new attitudes, behavior, and relationships.
• It provides personal and social rituals.

As you can see, besides dealing with problems, dance therapy nurtures a strong and healthy sense of self that supports the person as he faces issues in daily life.

Here is one way to adapt the journey improv toward therapeutic ends. Its goal is to explore responses, images, and feelings about the idea of going out on one's own, to present alternatives between the safety of known, well-defined areas and the willingness to explore new places independently and cope with unexpected obstacles which may crop up along the way. Allow sufficient time between the various instructions for responses to develop.

Journey (for therapy)
You are going on a journey. Find a starting place. Close your eyes; imagine yourself in a small, quiet space; there is little room for moving. How does that feel—safe and comfortable, or tight and restricting? Something starts moving in one part of your body. Notice the quality, speed, energy, or shape of the motion. It may be cool or warm, steady or erratic. Try to get a clearer sense of it as it travels to other parts of your body. Is it an intruder or is it welcome? Respond accordingly.

By some means, it is going to motivate you to leave your starting place. Are you going far or staying nearby? Going with hesitation and resolve, or eager restlessness and anticipation? Do any images come to mind? If so, allow them to affect your re-actions. Where have you moved to, and what is this new place like? Is the ground jagged or smooth, the air heavy or light? Are there wide vistas or narrow, confining cubicles? How do you feel about being there? Investigate this a bit.

Uh oh, something's just gotten in your way. What is it like? Big or small, delicate or brutal? Is it taking on any connotations? How will you deal with it? You could get past it, mesh with it, destroy it, partner it. How do you feel about that? empowered? weakened? resigned? relieved? angry? content? tired? Resolve your interaction with it in any way that's suitable. Either return to where you began, or end in another place. When you get there, make a final movement statement and bring your journey to an end. Stay for a few moments. Think back over the experience you just had and recall the things that were the most meaningful to you.

Discussion (you may want to have the movers sketch or write about this experience in their journals before the discussion): How did you begin? What about the place you were in? How did it feel? Did it remind you of anything in particular? a person? a situation? concern? Where in your body did the movement start? Might that have any particular significance? Was there anything important about how you left the starting place? How did you feel about that? What got in your way and how did you handle it? Were you ready to end at the ending? Why or why not? What was the most important part of this improv for you?

In review, notice how all the progressions in the improv are couched in open-ended terms, offering a wide range of alternatives. This is imperative, since our goal is to allow each person to control the experience and its exploration according to his own needs and perceptions. Throughout the improv, the mover is asked to attend to how he *feels* about what is happening, that is, how it is affecting his internal state. The relationship among movement image, perception, and affect is an important factor in working therapeutically. Repeatedly, this improv anchors the mover's awareness in his body's physical response rather than in words. This is a fundamental device, applicable not only in movement therapy, but in all movement improvisation, for it directs perception away from the mind and toward the body, where subconscious, intuitive associations and knowings are quietly and unwittingly ready to be called forth.

We hope that this short overview of dance improvisation in dance therapy will help you to understand its potential for bringing about change, so you are not surprised when you find yourself dealing with the therapeutic aspects of an improv aimed at different goals. Again, we caution you not to take on the mantle of a therapist, for to do so without the proper training is irresponsible.[7]

This chapter shows the way a central improv idea can be adapted to a variety of situations, and how improvisation can serve a variety of people whose backgrounds, talents, limitations, needs, and concerns differ widely. It also demonstrates that art, education, and therapy, while looking out on different streets, share a contiguous backyard through improvisation.

---

[7]Suggested reading: Penny L. Bernstein, *Eight Theoretical Approaches in Dance-Movement Therapy* (Dubuque, Iowa: Kendall-Hunt, 1979); Harris Chaiklin, ed., *Marian Chace: Her Papers* (available through the American Dance Therapy Association); Irmgard Bartenieff and Dori Lewis, *Body Movement: Coping with the Environment* (New York: Gordon and Breach, 1980); Mary Starks Whitehouse, "Physical Movement and Personality," *Contact Quarterly*, Winter 1987; Gilda Frantz, "An Approach to the Center: An Interview with Mary Whitehouse," *Psychological Perspectives*, Spring 1972; and Trudi Schoop, *Won't You Join the Dance?*

13 Academic Issues

One of the constant battles we face in higher education is making the study of dance academically respectable. The belief of modern dancers that a dancer's education should address the mind and creative faculties as well as the body has led to courses in dance notation and dance history. These courses have done wonders for our academic image. But realistically speaking, trying to convince the dean or the chair of the geology department, sitting on an academic review panel, that dance improvisation warrants any credit is another thing.

How does improvisation fit into an academic dance curriculum? Should it be a separate course or should it be incorporated into previously established ones? Does it have a specific body of knowledge? And if so, is it worthy of credit or only as useful as a sideline— an important endeavor but not equal to such disciplines as literature, biophysics, and Italian? These are all valid questions.

Dance improvisation is an integral part of the art of dance and as such is a valid subject for study. This book attests to the worth of improv and we hope that it, along with current research on the creative process and multiple intelligence, will add to the body of literature and give increased academic substance to the study of improvisation in many mediums.

In the meantime let's look at what can be accomplished in the study of dance improv.

After one semester, the improviser should be able to:
- Respond to a given stimulus in improvised movement.
- Create a basic organic form (beginning-middle-end).
- Know the difference between arbitrary and honest responses and how to suspend the former and allow the latter.
- Utilize the possibilities the body has for making movement statements.
- Articulate the appropriate use of space, time, and energy for the specific improv.

154

• Be open to a wide range of response: kinesthetic, emotional, intuitive, and intellectual.
• Have the confidence to maintain a solo and the ability to respond to other people in the intimate one-to-one relation of a duet and in the more complex relations of a trio and a quartet.
• Submerge himself in a larger group and move as one with nine or ninety-nine others.
• Keep in touch with the overall direction of the improv.
• Develop the movement material so that the improv is all about one thing and not a collection of diverse responses.

In a second semester course, the student would enlarge these skills and learn to:
• Capitalize on internal phrasing and transitions to create an articulate internal form that supports the overall form.
• Incorporate contrast and variety while maintaining an overall direction and intention.
• Identify, analyze, and appreciate the very wide range of various movement styles and emotional/philosophical responses of different individuals.
• Create his own improvs.
• Become aware of the various potential uses for improvisation as a tool in technique, choreography, therapy, creative pursuits, and performance.

An advanced class that included readings, lectures, and discussions would bring many of the above skills to a more cognitive level and develop an understanding of the medium of movement and how it comes into play in dance improv and as a part of the creative process.

Besides the actual experience of improv there are academic activities that can augment the improv experience. Use the following according to the amount of credit given and the level of the course (lower or upper division, graduate level).

Journal. Record your objective and subjective experiences and observations. In writing up an improv consider what happened:
• Record physical sensations and images.
• Describe intriguing movement/moments.
• Comment on specific relationships and the identity of the group.

- Identify potential applications (Can you use what happened for choreography?).
- Investigate how you felt about the group as well as about the improv itself.
- Explore how the material which developed in the improv relates to yourself and to the rest of your life.
- State problems and suggest solutions.
  Also look at the compositional elements:
- Was the form of the improv clear and decisive?
- Did any one element (space, time, energy) become the subject of the improv? Or did it strongly support a dramatic idea?
- Was abstraction a predominant factor? If so, how?
- Did the movement take on a particular style?
  And consider the improv:
- What was its goal?
- Did it work?
- How else could it have been presented? Discuss pacing.
- Would you want more instructions or fewer?
- More images or fewer?

Let the improv inspire a poem, a sketch, some original music, a graph, a sculpture.

(The journal can be collected every week or twice a semester. As leader, you should give written feedback with support, questions, and challenges. For the best results *allow class time for writing in the journal* in addition to assigning it as homework. If your students want to keep a detailed record of the improvs, that's fine, but that is not the purpose of the journal. The journal is about the experience itself. If an improv was not particularly interesting for them they should so state and not feel obliged to write further. Instead they should spend their time assessing and investigating the improvs where something enriching did happen. When the journal is written by dance therapy students, the observations and analysis will be specifically guided by therapeutic concerns and will revolve more around movement as metaphor for problems, analysis of patients' responses, breakthroughs, fears, and resistances.)

Movement profile. Work up a personal movement profile including the following and remembering also to take observations from your daily life into account. Do you mainly use high or low energy, lots of space or little? Do you move fast or slow? Are your territorial instincts strong (consider your relationship to your roommate as well to the improv group)? What are your favorite gestures? How do you sleep—all over the place or in a tight unmoving ball? Notice how your walking posture and tempo are influenced by your moods. Where do you carry your tension—shoulders, jaw...? Notice how you relate to others. Do you touch others easily? Are you willing to be touched? If you were an animal, which animal are you most like? Which would you *like* to be?

Write a movement profile on someone you see a lot every day—a friend, teacher, or family member. Use the above questions to structure your observations.

Improv profiles. In improv how do you move? Which is your favorite movement quality? Your favorite movement? What do you never do? Do you prefer to follow or lead? What type of improv material are you most comfortable responding to, dramatic or abstract? Solo, partner, or group? What do you think is the place of music in dance improv? What is the most difficult aspect about improvising for you? How do you usually deal with it? Think up three possible solutions and try them out. How did they work? Do we improvise in daily life? (What about when being cross-examined about a lie?) Use your experience in class to define *improv.*

A creative project. Collect stimuli for movement, a scrapbook or bag of places to begin.
• A list of movement-oriented words: action words, qualities, images, poetry, stories, myths, characters, feelings, moods.
• Paintings and photographs, both abstract and realistic.
• Sculpture, objects from nature, found objects.
• Music and sound: records, tapes, instruments, homemade instruments.
• Movement: a motif to develop, a floor pattern, a beginning formation, three movements to use as the main ingredient.
• Written instructions for a variety of improvs, including possibilities for solos or for small and large groups.

Lead an improv. Create and lead your own improv and the ensuing discussion. Write your own evaluation.

Research report. Research and write a report and/or oral presentation on any aspect of dance improv. Lead an improv that you create specifically from the material of your report. Lead the discussion afterward, getting feedback on the improv in relation to the report as well as to how it stood on its own.

Possibilities for reports include the use of improv in dance therapy; how choreographers use improvisation as a primary component in their choreography or performance; dance improv and trance dance in another culture; improv and the creative process.

Grading is a fact of academic life. Grading the experiential part of an improv class is not simple; achievement is not readily quantified. If the course content is all studio work, a non-credit or a pass/fail system works well. Or you may simply state at the beginning of the course that prompt and regular attendance will yield everyone a B. This lays to rest concerns about "How well am I doing in terms of a grade?" and lets the process of improvisation live for itself rather than for some negotiable grade-god. Of course, if journals, research papers, or presentations are required then the improv experience is only one of several elements to be considered.

The following criteria for grading a final exam use behavioral objectives. They are useful for the dean's files, the State Board of Regents, or similar administrative bodies, but they may just help you think about the rather strange situation of giving an *exam* in improv. They can also be considered as course objectives and given to the students at the beginning of the course.

1. Given an improvisation with the following possibilities (solo, duet, small group, large group) and the following range of stimuli (a given dynamic, quality, a specific piece of music, a physical object, another person, an abstract concept or symbol), the learner is able to become honestly and creatively involved and keep the integrity of the theme while performing an improvisation that has inherent organic form.

2. After performing in, or observing, an improvisation, the student is able to discuss it with honesty, integrity, and discrimination.

If you are requiring journals, projects, papers, or exams on the conceptual aspects of improv, include them in the criteria as well.

14 Sources

Now that we have looked at the *act* of improvisation, what of the content? What can a leader use as the basic sources for developing an improv? Posing such a question is like asking for a list of the names of the stars in the universe. The problem is (1) they don't all have names; (2) they aren't all known; (3) more are always in the process of being created. Yet we can establish certain units and categories and then show some examples of improvs which could be developed within those categories. A list prepared by someone else would undoubtedly take a different form. We offer this organization simply to get you started. For those of you who already have more ideas than time to try them out, skip this chapter and use the time for just that purpose.[1]

Unit 1. Trust and Relaxation
Unit 2. Individual Growth Schema (using an individual's psychological growth and social interaction)
    Self to Inner Self
    Self to Outer Self
    Self to Important Other
    Self as Part of the Group
    Self to the World
Unit 3. Sensory Awakening (using the perceptive, receptive, and expressive senses)
    Kinesthesia
    Touch
    Sight
    Hearing
    Speech
    Smell and Taste

---

[1]A number of improvs and exercises in this chapter appear also in our previous book, *The Intimate Act of Choreography*. We repeat them here because they serve a basic purpose that can be developed either toward the craft of choreography or skill in improvisation.

Unit 4. Elements of Movement
 Space
 Time
 Energy
 Movement and Movement Qualities
Unit 5. Composition (using the processes of giving structure)
 Phrasing
 Overall Form
 Transitions
 Manipulation
 Abstraction
 Symbols
Unit 6. Accompaniment (capitalizing on the use of sound, especially music)
Unit 7. Theatrics (incorporating additional material beyond the physical bodies of the movers, such as props, masks, costumes, lights, sets)
Unit 8. Art Forms (using literature, visual art, photography, film, drama, dance, music, and other art forms)
Unit 9. Social Behavior (using gestures, customs, rituals, myths, taboos, and culturally conditioned assumptions)

For each category, we provide a succinct description of several improvs, in no particular order. Since the categories are not mutually exclusive, an improv is often applicable to several. Therefore, after each improv, we indicate in italics the other categories (or entire units) it could serve. As you use the various improvs for different purposes, make the necessary adjustments in emphasis.

Following each category is (1) a list of Other Applicable Improvs, which are given in this book and can be located by using the index; and (2) a list of Improv Ideas, which should be sufficiently self-explanatory and provocative to stimulate ideas. When the crossover is not immediately obvious or requires some adaptation, we offer some explanations and suggestions.

Some individual improvs could be developed so as to provide enough material for several improvisations or sessions; others could spawn whole new subcategories (see, for example, **Body Systems** in Self to Inner Self). Some improvs are more like games **(Elephant**

Game) while still others (An Object) incorporate standard imagination or lateral thinking exercises and stimulate greater invention by orienting one to look with a new eye and respond with a fresh attitude. Rather than separate out such exercises, we include them within their appropriate categories to add choice, variety, and breadth to both the material and the process.

The improv suggestions also cover many levels of response. For example, **Machine Make-a-Sound** will not produce a profound level of response, because both the content and structure suggest a rather limited depth of involvement. However, it is precisely because of its straightforward simplicity that it might be appropriate under certain circumstances; it is nonthreatening and easily accessible. Other improvs, such as **The Big Hum** or the **Journey (for therapy)** (see chapter 12, "Specific Populations") are designed to produce quite a deep level of attunement, response, and possible self-confrontation. The choice of which type of improv is appropriate for a given group at a given time is obviously determined by the leader.

Unit 1. Trust and Relaxation

Before we address the main body of improvs, let's look at some exercises and improvs that work on relaxation and build trust. Their aim is to create a responsive, receptive interaction among the participants.

Some of these, although they stimulate awareness and kinetic discovery, do not result in a lot of original, creative movement. The trust exercises, however, are particularly useful for getting beginners oriented in their bodies, comfortable with others, and aware of the kinesthetic boundaries they can feel safe in. They also are important in developing good working relationships among people in a newly formed group. We suggest that because of their preparatory nature, some trust improvs be among your early improv offerings. The relaxation exercises provide a welcome treat either after some particularly exhausting improvisatory work, or during a time (such as final exams or performances) when tension and fatigue levels are running high.

Trust Circle
In a circle, shoulder to shoulder, facing in; one person in the center, eyes closed, feet rooted to the ground and body kept in one

unit (not bending at the waist, hips, or knees). Center person tilts to the front, side, and back; people on the perimeter support him, shifting him around and across the circle. As trust builds, allow the person to tilt further before catching him. Note: Although everyone is responsible for the falling person, distribute the stronger people evenly around the circle for safety in catching him. When he begins to get very low it may need four people at a time to keep him moving safely. (*Self as Part of the Group; Kinesthesia*)

The Lift
One person lies on his back. Everyone puts hands on him, gripping tightly for ten counts; take ten counts to release. Very slowly lift him overhead; walk; undulate his body as if it was floating on waves. Very slowly, lower. Put hands on very lightly, ten counts to tighten; then ten counts to lighten and off. Have the person say how it felt.

Back-to-Back
Sit in pairs, back to back, spines touching, eyes closed. Can you feel your partner breathing? Begin to move and get to know the other person through his back. Allow yourself to be supported and to support. One of you tell your partner a story, joke, or secret using only your back. Switch roles. Talk about what happened. Note: Good for beginners; a great ice-breaker. (*Self to Important Other; Touch*)

Mirroring
One person mirrors the movement of another. Note what's easiest to follow (slow motion, facing each other). Leader calls out the changes of leadership; the changes become faster and faster until the movement takes on a life of its own as the leader stops calling the changes. Note: This is a classic and is important for beginners. (*Self to Important Other; Sight*)

Duet Balance—Standing
Partners face one another, feet together, toes touching. They hold hands and both lean backward, establishing an equilibrium; each

must pull back in order to provide the counterweight for the other. Note: This is a version of the type of improvs often found in Contact Improvisation and demonstrates the gains possible when two people are truly interdependent. (A short discussion of Contact Improvisation may be found in chapter 6, "Formats.")

Blind Milling

Eyes closed. Movement exploration relying on senses other than sight. Encourage interaction when it happens. Find a partner without using sight and sit down facing each other. One at a time, explore your partner's face by touch. Try to identify who it is. (*Touch; Space*; unit 9, *Social Behavior*)

Pair Walk

In twos. Side by side, put up your inside hand as a blinder so you can't see your partner; begin walking directly across the room; one person determines starts and stops while the other tries to match identically. The walk must include starts, stops, changes in speed, forward and backward directions (but not sideways). Switch roles. Repeat again without either person being identified as the determiner so the pair must be mutually attentive and responsive. Note: May be repeated a number of times during the term with the same partner as a way of seeing if familiarity with the other's movement patterns increases intuitive sensing mechanisms. (*Self to Important Other*)

Blind Mirroring

In twos. Sit facing each other, eyes closed; begin with palms lightly touching, then move them slightly away; try to mirror each other. (*Self to Important Other*)

Stomach Laugh

Lie down in a staircase floor pattern with each person's head on the stomach of the person before them. Person at one end arbitrarily begins to laugh; then the next one (at first this will be artificial—that will change soon enough). Allow to evolve as it will. Note: Good tension releaser. (*Self as Part of the Group*; unit 6, *Accompaniment*)

Create-a-Trust

In groups of two, three, or four, create a physical situation where one person needs to physically trust the others as in being carried, thrown, caught, or jumped over. Show the rest of the group. Discuss your apprehensions and talk about how they were or could have been eased. Try again. Note: Stress that safety is everyone's responsibility; there is no trust without it. *(Self as Part of the Group)*

The Cloud

Lying down on your back, eyes closed. An imaginary cloud enters through the window and advances from your toes up toward your head, gradually obscuring and enveloping your body, making you light. Then it rises with you in it and exits through the window and out into the sky. *(Self to Inner Self; Kinesthesia)*

Relax by Half

Lying down on your back, eyes closed. Contract one part of body as much as possible, then let half the tension release, then half again, then half again, half again, and finally release it all. Do with individual parts of body and then in combinations. Repeat using cross-lateral parts (e.g., left leg and right arm), and then with the whole body. *(Self to Inner Self; Kinesthesia)*

Tension Plop

Same as above but allow the force of the contraction to lift the body part slightly off the ground. Leader urges "stronger, harder, hold the tension." Then on leader's clap, release tension all at once and let that part drop to the floor. *(Self to Inner Self; Kinesthesia)*

Tension Release Walk

(Preparation: Standing, become limp, passive; experience the weight of your own body, give in to gravity.) Begin walking around the room. Notice where there is any tension; release it. Search for other spots of tension and release them. After a while you'll notice that it takes tension just to continue walking; release that also and gradually collapse. *(Kinesthesia)*

Lifting

Use demonstration format. Working in twos one person lies on his back, heavy, passive. Partner lifts part of body and gently moves it around, encouraging release. Start with the smaller parts of the body (e.g., lower arm) and move on to larger parts (entire leg). Notice if the passive person is assisting or resisting with the lifts; point this out to him. Switch roles. Note: Remind lifters that they are responsible for their partners. *(Self to Important Other; Kinesthesia)*

Unit 2. Individual Growth Schema
Self to Inner Self

Breathing

Work with different breath patterns: (1) slow inhale and exhale; (2) panting; (3) slow inhale, quick exhale ("Hah!"); (4) quick inhale (gasp), slow hiss out; (5) quick inhale, hold, quick exhale. Experiment with corresponding movement in different parts of the body and in the whole body, with partial breaths. Note: Can be helpful in developing a sense of phrasing. *(Time; Phrasing; Overall Form; unit 6, Accompaniment)*

Elastic

Imagine elastic bands between body parts. Stretch and release. Vary the elastic's length and tensile strength. Also try real elastics. Note: Good for beginners and for children. *(Self to Important Other; Self as Part of the Group)*

Twist to Whirl

Twist isolated parts of the body; vary directions and speed. Increase until whole body is twisting and/or whirling. (You can spot a number of places in the room or your hand.) Note: Some people have a great deal of trouble with continuous turning which does not get better with practice. *(Kinesthesia; Movement and Movement Qualities)*

Open-Close

Open and close a part of your body; the whole body. Consider what you open to, close away from, or close around. Observe how open or closed you become. *(Space)*

Internal Landscape
Eyes closed, lying down. Give the following description. "Your body is hollow; there is a strong searchlight exploring your body from the inside. Start in your head and progress through your entire body. [Allow plenty of time for this.] Switch awareness to the body surface as it exudes warmth and energy. Is an aura surrounding you? How far does the aura extend? Is it complete? If not, where are the gaps? Explore that area in movement. What color is the aura? Does it vibrate, come in waves, or tiny explosions? Move it. Incorporate the whole body in the movement." Note: There is no movement for the first part of this improv.

Balance
Experiment with different and unusual ways of balancing, using various parts of the body to lean on or balance with. Experiment by moving and then abruptly stopping or interrupting a natural phrase, forcing the balance to occur in an unlikely position. Do not think of balance as stasis; also, you can be moving some body parts while balanced on others. *(Kinesthesia)*

Body Systems
Use the different body systems (circulatory, glandular, nervous, mechanical, respiratory) as material. The leader must be familiar with the operation of these systems and their movement correlatives. Note: This can be used as a way to add some basic kinesiological information to an improv class.

Emotions
Leader designates a movement that corresponds to an emotion (e.g., rocking the body for comfort from grief, a powerful punch for anger), then gives movement instructions only, not identifying the emotion. In the discussion see if the emotions emerged from the movement. Note: This can lead to a deep level of response, triggering blocked information, and resistances. Watch for this and

either end with some positive emotions or provide an exit from the negative ones. Allow time for discussion.

Other Applicable Improvs (for page numbers see index)
Relax by Half
Tension Plop
The Cloud
Turned In—Turned Out
Still Shape
Suspend, Fall, and Recovery

Improv Ideas
private space
enter own body
tape worm
stretching
favorite dream/worst nightmare
umbilical cord
shrinking/expanding
uptight

Self to Outer Self

Self-Touch
Part touched becomes focal point for movement exploration.
Note: Very simple.

Part-of-Body Conversation
Conversation between different body parts; may be an argument, a soothing exchange, a formal encounter, a telling of a joke, or an attraction/repulsion duet.

Point Base
Leader calls out a number. Movers may have that many points of contact with the ground. Explore design and movement given that restriction. Option: Point of contact with someone else may be substituted for one or more ground contacts. Note: Fun.
(Space)

Carry Yourself

Try to completely release the weight of one body part and carry it with another (e.g., carry head with wrist). Experiment with different parts being the lifter and the lifted. (Emphasizes sensation of weight and especially of being active and passive at the same time.) Note: Tricky. *(Kinesthesia)*

Part of Body

(1) One body part initiates a movement which then spreads to other parts. (2) One body part functions as the lead with the rest of the body following along (include a variety of directions, levels, and use of energy). (3) One body part begins a simple movement (a trembling, an up/down/around pattern), which is continuously repeated; the rest of the body explores other possibilities while that continues.

Going

This should be given as a one-word instruction for an entire improv; it is very open-ended.

Hiding

Specify certain areas of the body to cover up; explore movement possibilities while keeping that part hidden (the part may be hidden from one particular vantage point or from everywhere). *(Self to the World; unit 9, Social Behavior)*

Shadows

Done in the dark with a single light source in the room—flashlight, lamp, stage light. Let the shadows be the dance. Place the light source at different angles and different distances from the mover. Try two isolated light sources. *(Sight; Space; unit 7, Theatrics)*

Extremities

Emphasize and explore the movement possibilities of the extremities of the body.

Tiny Parts

Small movement with small body parts (tongue, toe, belly button). *(Space)*

Distortions

Work with spatial irregularities: twisting, askew alignment, hunch-back, sickled feet, a limp; try it in place and traveling. Or work with an actual or imagined limitation: stiff leg, hands tied behind your back, wrist tied to ankle. Try some random abrupt accents, a recurring pattern that doesn't really belong with the rest of the movement: a tick, a twitch. Note: Although this is especially useful for people who are overly involved with pretty movement, it is excellent for everyone because it takes them into a new realm of movement. (*Space*)

Faces

Begin with a facial expression; make a movement pattern with your face (with or without accompanying sound). Allow body posture and movement to develop. Repeat a number of times adding more and more body movement. Try different faces. Note: The group may resist this one at first, but once they get into it, it's wild and wonderful. (Unit 9, *Social Behavior*)

Right/Left Discrimination

Leader calls out instructions with increasingly rapid changes. Instructions include body parts, side of body, and movement or movement quality. Develop into simultaneous instructions for several body parts (flutter your left hip while you swing your right arm as you stomp across the room to the left of the door). Note: This throws some kinks into the usual patterns that people follow. Lateral discrimination is a classic ingredient in the development of body-image and in coordination facility. (*Kinesthesia; Movement and Movement Qualities*)

Name

Write out your name with your hip; while traveling. Print it; write it in cursive; backward. Note: Simple. Short. Great for children. (*Abstraction*)

With a Mind of Its Own

Different parts of your body seem to go their own way, to the annoyance or even horror of the rest. Note: Can be developed humorously.

Schizoid
Give two opposing instructions for different body parts (e.g., top half strong—bottom half light; right side, tender—left side, angry). Note: This can be quite difficult and frustrating.

Gestures
Pick a gesture that relates to the self: grooming (adjusting hair), a nervous tick (eyes blinking, fingers tapping), reassurance (hand to mouth, arms akimbo, self hug). Use the gesture as the basis of an improv. A possibility: transfer the timing and energy of eyes blinking to different parts of the body. Note: This is for experienced movers because the movement resulting from the gesture may be too subtle to occur to a beginner. Certainly wait until after doing the section on manipulations. (Unit 9, *Social Behavior*)

Postures
(Preparation: Bring in pictures of a single person in which the posture strongly says something about the person. These can be found in advertisements, works of art, family photo albums, textbooks, newspapers, and magazines. Look at all the pictures. Discuss how the *body*, without the facial expression, makes the statement. Use **A Position** as a preparation.) Pick one posture and use it as the theme of your improv. (Unit 8, *Art Forms*; unit 9, *Social Behavior*)

Kinespheres
Exploration of near, intermediate, and far space (*near* is the range of movement possible when you are in a cylinder no larger than your body; *intermediate* increases your spatial access to the size of a phone booth; for *far*, turn yourself into a space glutton, reaching and affecting as much space as possible from an anchored place). In each of these three spaces, vary the movement experience by suggesting changes in timing; by working from a sitting, kneeling, or lying position; or by moving through space. Have the group pay attention to the emotional and dramatic associations that each variation produces. Note: Read the work of Edward Hall and Rudolf von Laban, noted movement analysts, for greater under-

standing of this aspect of human behavior. (*Space*; unit 9, *Social Behavior*)

Human Evolution
Begin as a blob on the floor. Progress from an amoeba to a two-celled animal, to a flatworm.... Become more differentiated, articulated. Progress from random wiggling to purposeful crawling, from belly, to four-footedness, to upright. Progress from hesitation to surety, to control, to freedom, to refinement and cooperation. (*Movement and Movement Qualities; Transitions*)

Becoming Civilized
Start with indirect and accommodating movements (circular, flexible, erratic, playful); these gradually become direct and manipulative, strong, regulated, and unyielding. This ultimately leads to increased limitations on the movement until it becomes stifled and repetitive. (*Movement and Movement Qualities*; unit 9, *Social Behavior*)

Flight
Begin with a sense of being grounded, bulky, heavy, earthbound. Focus is downward, movement is anchored, gravity is prominent. Focus shifts to eye level and locomotion is explored. Gradually focus ascends; notice the flying creatures. Try to grasp for them, emulate them, become them; be airborne and light; fly. Note: This could develop from **Human Evolution** by adding flight to the progression given there. (*Space; Movement and Movement Qualities*)

Personal Style.   See chapter 9, "Advanced Challenges."

Other Applicable Improvs (for page numbers see index)
Impulse/Follow-through
As Clay (using one's own body)
Body Contours
Picture Pose
Planes

Positive/Negative
A Position
Poems

Improv Ideas
bouncing
oiling joints
ritual (cleansing, decoration)
kinetic sculpture
figure/ground
throw away part of body
I am an instrument

Self to Important Other

Most of these are duets. Many call for repetition with the partners switching roles. These should be preceded by the two basic improvs, **Back-to-Back** and **Mirroring,** given in unit 1, *Trust and Relaxation.*

Conversation I
Have a movement dialogue, each person starting with a different kind of movement (e.g., slow, sustained vs. fast, abrupt; or strong vs. gentle).

Conversation II
One person speaks (moves); the other answers (also in movement); then the first one moves in response to that answer; and so on. Soon both are moving somewhat continuously in response to each other. You can listen as you move and move as you listen; there is no need to stop moving to know what the other person is saying. (Unit 9, *Social Behavior*)

Conversation III
Start with mirroring; let it evolve into an interaction.

The Encounter
Pairs begin at opposite ends of the room. Walk toward and past your partner three times: (1) with eye contact at some point during

the crossing; (2) with eye contact from the beginning and with physical contact of any sort when passing; (3) as above but allow movement interaction to develop fully before resolving and leaving. (Unit 9, *Social Behavior*)

Supports
Experiment with different ways of lifting, supporting, or carrying each other's weight or body parts (you do not have to lift the entire body). Explore these from a stationary position and while traveling. The lifter should perceive himself as helpmate and caretaker; he has the responsibility for his partner. Note: Helps develop a sense of mutuality. (*Kinesthesia*; unit 9, *Social Behavior*)

Up/Down
One person investigates movement on the ground while the other pursues complementary or responsive movement on a higher level. With or without locomotion. (*Space*)

Including
(Preparation: **Kinesphere**) Duet. Start alone, using near space; after a while change to intermediate and far space, incorporating your partner.

Shadowing
Duet. Face the same way, one person behind the other. Shadow her movement. Be as identical as possible. Try again from across the floor. Note: Excellent for observing details in movement.

Open Duet
Do a duet.

As a Duet
Do any duet. After a while, staying as a unit, work with other couples.

Freeze!
In threes or fours. Two people do a duet; the others watch. One

calls "Freeze!" and then replaces one of the movers. The duet continues with the new person *taking on the movement and intent of the one he replaced.*

Directing a Duet
See chapter 9, "Advanced Challenges." Also see the discussion of Contact Improv in chapter 6, "Formats."

Other Applicable Improvs (for page numbers see index)
Back-to-Back
Mirroring
Duet Balance—Standing
Pair Walk
Blind Mirroring
Lifting
Elastic (in twos)
Freeze Duet
Gestures (in twos, using paired gestures, and postures, e.g., an embrace, an attack)
Take Down
Positive and Negative Charge
Suspend, Fall, and Recovery (allow suspension to occur with eye or physical contact with partner)
Turned In/Turned Out
As Clay
Voice/Movement Conversation
A Type of Touch
Positive/Negative (create the designs as a duet)
Three Punches
Toss
Accumulations Minus One
Passing By
As One
Photography

Improv Ideas
lead/follow
the challenge

push me—pull you
give and take
fingertips
confrontation
contact and lack of
siamese twins
sparring
wrestling
cooperation
task collaboration
so far away, yet as one

Self as Part of the Group

Progressive Mural
Emphasize two-dimensional design. One person takes a shape up
against a wall. Anyone else goes up and adds on her shape, en-
larging the mural. The addition may be with or without contact
but must be on same plane and relate visually or thematically to
what is already there. Attend to levels and proximity differences.
When half of the group has created the mural, rest of the group
goes up and takes their places so the makers can see what they
have created. Note: Good for beginners. (*Space; Sight;* unit 8, *Art
Forms*)

Progressive Sculpture
Same as above, but in three-dimensional form. (*Sight; Space;* unit
8, *Art Form*)

Progressive Sound
One person begins in center of a circle with any repetitive move-
ment and a corresponding, repetitive sound. Another adds on
with his own sound and movement that augments the first one.
Continue till the whole group is participating. (*Hearing; Speech;
Time;* unit 6, *Accompaniment*)

Trio/Quartet
Create a short repetitive movement. Do it in unison until it evolves
into a trio or quartet.

Tilt Together
Standing in a crowd or in a circle with the sides of their bodies touching, the group as a whole begins to tilt, side to side. Allow to evolve. Repeat, beginning with a vibration.

Explosions
Work with the idea of explosions of energy between people. Pay attention to the energy buildup. Begin to build clusters of people exploding together. The goal is to get one explosion to happen simultaneously for the entire group. Note: For experienced movers. Good for building group unity. *(Energy; Movement and Movement Qualities)*

As You Pass
Have people travel curved paths (large curves that coil around the room, tiny ornamental arcs and circles), with their bodies reflecting the sinuous floor patterns. Be aware of others passing. At first come close but don't touch; then touch on the passing (touching hands, rolling off backs, shoulders, and heads). Stay awhile and develop the contact before passing on to another. Trios and quartets are fine. Note: Good for beginners.

Together
Start with an easy run in a counterclockwise circle. (Leader joins the running and works with the group for the next sequence.) Slow down, face in, do chassé sideways. Slower; walk, do grape-vine step to the right (side-front, side-back). Bend the body forward on the front step, up for the others. Let the steps be weighted and easy. Keep repeating. (Leader steps out and the circle closes up.) Continue this until, as a group, you find where it leads. *(Overall Form)*

Confrontation
Two groups establish their own identity, using a simple movement quality, pattern, and/or formation (e.g., in a tightly knit group, twist into self and each other). Once the group is established they, as a whole, confront the other group. Try it with three or four groups. Note: For experienced movers. (Unit 9, *Social Behavior*)

Elephant Game

An obstacle course is set up by an outsider, where the group cannot see it. The group chooses a leader. The leader is shown the route through the course and then attempts to bring the group safely through. The leader can see but cannot talk or vocalize; the rest of the group can talk but cannot see (keep eyes closed or be blindfolded). The outsider can be present and do anything he wants to stymie the group. The group, in a planning session, may decide upon any device or signal to use between them, and their leader (e.g., claps for yes/no, left/right, high/low). The outsider may identify the signals and use them to give inappropriate feedback to the group. Note: This can really get group dynamics going. (Unit 7, *Theatrics*; unit 9, *Social Behavior*)

A Gift

In a circle, take four steps in, hold two counts, take four steps back, turn around (four counts), bend slightly forward and back up (four counts). Repeat. This should be done with a sense of ritual; bring something in (an offering), or take something away (strength, a more distinctive identity). As a group, decide where you want it to go. Note: This is a good closing ritual for the last class of the term. (Unit 8, *Art Forms*; unit 9, *Social Behavior*)

Order—Chaos—Order

Leader puts the group in a distinct formation (wedge) and gives a simple, formal movement combination. Repeat the combination until the precision begins to weaken and the formation to deteriorate. It may happen by way of a softness in the body, variations in the movement, or a lingering or speeding up of the timing. Let it go for a while until it has reached a certain degree of anarchy or chaos then gradually bring it back to order. It can be the original order, some variation of it, or something completely different (but it must resume some identifiable order). Note: For experienced movers. *(Overall Form)*

Roar In

In a circle, facing in. Go toward and away from the center, each time making the inward movement higher in excitement, pitch, and

fervor. Establish a communion of the group, and allow any resolution or development that occurs. Try with sound. Note: This
improv works nicely at the end of a session to provide a sense of
unity, completion, and ensemble. It can be quite short or it can be
the beginning of an extended improv. (*Transitions*; unit 9, *Social
Behavior*)

Take Down
Mill around. One person brings another to the ground. Try different
ways of taking people down; the one being taken can assist, resist,
or be passive. Once he is down, let him stay there, or take him
back up. Continue to mill. Once down you can get up by yourself or wait for someone to take you up. Note: Good for beginners.
(*Self to Important Other*; unit 9, *Social Behavior*)

Positive and Negative Charge
(1) In twos. Have specific parts of your body drawn toward or re-
pelled from specific parts of your partner's body. Let the charge
(positive or negative), the degree of power, and the body parts
change as often as you wish. (2) Mill around the room. Same as
above except you can work with anyone in the room including
someone across the room who does not know that you are working
with them. Consider working off two people at the same time.
(*Self to Important Other*)

Rhythm Circle   See chapter 5, "Leader's Concerns." (*Overall
Form*; *Symbols*; unit 6, *Accompaniment*; unit 9, *Social Behavior*)

Poison   See chapter 11, "Behavioral Problems" (*Space*, unit 9, *Social Behavior*)

For Fifty   See chapter 9, "Advanced Challenges."

Trading Focus   See chapter 9, "Advanced Challenges." (*Overall
Form*; unit 9, *Social Behavior*)

Break-out   See chapter 9, "Advanced Challenges."

Amoeba   See chapter 8, "Create Your Own Improv." Note: For experienced movers.

Out and In Again   See chapter 9, "Advanced Challenges."

Other Applicable Improvs (for page numbers see index)
Trust Circle
Blind Milling
Stomach Laugh
Create-a-Trust
Elastic (with entire group or small groups connected to a single
   huge elastic)
The Big Hum
Line
Sun Worship II
Name Chant
Toss (as a group)
Slow Changes
Photography (using group pictures)
Plays and Scenes from Literature (using group incidents)
Mise-en-Scène (for a group)
A Goddess or a God
Hello/Good-bye
Games
Days of Knights and Ladies

Improv Ideas
in and out the window
bumping
introductions
circle break-in/break-out
initiation ritual
the herd (or flocking)
territoriality
group project/group problem
Siamese quintuplets
yo heave ho

Self to the World

Nature
Use any natural forms or acts of nature for inspiration: insects, cloud patterns, gorges and waterfalls, storms, avalanches, rainbows, the upper branches of trees.

Explore a Chair
Investigate various ways of moving in, around, through, and with it. Turn it over; find ways of having it travel. Try this with any common object (table, stick, mirror, rope, garbage can). Note: Good for beginners. Also great for kids. (*Abstraction*; unit 7, *Theatrics*)

Imaginary Environment
Imagine yourself in a desert, traveling in a snowstorm, over jagged terrain, or in an environment or a specific energy or time field (the Twilight Zone). (*Movement and Movement Qualities*)

Environments
Consider going to different places to improvise: playground, cave, airport, beach, spiral staircase. Use the place itself to provide focus for the improv. Add other layers, contingencies, or intentions. Note: For experienced movers specifically, because it is done in public. Try an area with a low density population for the group's first experience, or one friendly to creative meanderings (e.g., the sculpture room or outer garden of an art museum). You may need to get permission first.

Multimedia
The leader creates a total environment for the participants, including sound, colors, lights, objects, smells. It may be real, imaginatively described, or a mixture of the two. Give instructions on how to approach the environment in movement. Possibly have them connect first with the most movement-producing aspect (e.g., it's slippery) and then incorporate the rest. Note: For experienced movers. This should be preceded by improvs that concentrate on

one aspect at a time, such as **Flashlight, Pick an Instrument, From the Past, Sets, Lights, In Costume.** (Unit 7, *Theatrics*; unit 8, *Art Forms*)

Room as Movement Score

Facing the wall, proceed clockwise around the room. The wall—its surface and all the things on or against it—serves as the movement score. Essentially, the movers read the room and respond to it. (For example, if you see an electrical outlet you can move as if your finger just jabbed into it, respond to its small rectangular flatness, or make any other connection.) Movers are free to bypass other movers; if they come into your visual field they become part of the score. Note: Helps heighten awareness of creative possibilities from things usually overlooked. Postmoderns will appreciate its ordinary base. (*Sight; Abstraction*)

Alone in the Studio

Before the group arrives, clear the studio space, turn off the lights (or leave one low light on), close the doors, and meet them outside. One at a time they enter the studio; alone, they are free to do anything they want, in complete privacy with no time limit. The rest wait silently. As each person finishes and comes out, they collect and wait until all the rest have had their turn. When everyone is finished, talk about it. Note: This works well at night and can be presented as a sanctifying of the studio space, maybe as the first class of a second term. It is *not* for beginners. It strengthens the movers' sense of special connection to the space they regularly work in. It would also work well on stage the night before tech week starts—they should be encouraged to work with the space and not practice their repertory.) (*Space*)

Machines

In small groups. Work out a movement interpretation of a machine, such as a lawn mower, clothes dryer, sewing machine, conveyer belt, or dump truck. Each group tries a different machine; show it to the others. Note: Good for children.

Fantasy Trip
Choose any place, real or imaginary, that you have always wanted to visit. Explore the getting there, being there, and leaving there.

Other Applicable Improvs (for page numbers see index)
Hiding
The Wall
Sets
Create an Environment
Poems
Journey

Improv Ideas
moonwalk
corners and windows
playground
open meadow
space odyssey
facing the faceless
environments, usual and otherwise
a place in the universe
past—present—future
out of the dark, into the light
microscopic to telescopic
the rise and fall
ascent or descent of man
untold treasures
transformations (try a variety)
locker room, print shops, and strange places

Unit 3. Sensory Awakening
Kinesthesia

The kinesthetic sense, often bypassed by the more externally apparent senses of taste, touch, sight, hearing and smell, is actually the most potent and relevant one for the dancer. It refers to the body's ability to perceive weight, balance, verticality, laterality, gravity, buoyancy, volume, muscular tension, fatigue, release, stretch, flex-

ion and extension, rotation, spatial orientation, and timing. Improvs
in this category need to be given in ways that stress the perception of
what is happening with the body and the use of that perception for
movement motivation.

Suspend, Fall, and Recovery

Suspension is the last point of balance prior to a release and fall.
Incorporate locomotion as an outcome of the fall. Let it take you
part way down, or all the way to the floor. Return to a point of
balance, then to suspension again. The balance need not stop
completely, nor always end in a standing position. Try it with
your eyes closed; note the difference. Note: Precede with **Trust
Circle.** Good for beginners and people whose dance background is
strongly anchored in the vertical, classical, ballet style. Good for
introducing the basic concept of Humphrey-Limón technique.
*(Self to Inner Self; Self to Important Other; Energy; Phrasing;
Transitions)*

Still Shape

Get into any shape; hold for thirty seconds. Feel where the muscular tensions are, the weight, the stretch, the balance. Use that
kinetic information to bring the still shape to life. Try another
shape, and another. *(Self to Inner Self; Space)*

Turned In/Turned Out

First work with inward and outward rotation of individual body
parts; then with turning the body as a whole into itself. Both in
place and while locomoting. As you approach and encounter other
people, notice accommodating or confrontational attitudes and
changing sense of self-image. Note: An important experience for
actors and therapy-oriented people, as it gives insight into the
relationship between physical and emotional states. *(Self to Inner
Self; Self to Important Other)*

Impulse/Follow-through

Use different body parts to initiate an impulse and a follow-
through. Vary the strength and duration of the impulses and the
follow-throughs. Try in duets, passing the energy impulse to your

partner; try it in close and from across the room. Allow the possibility of incorporating others into your toss game. Note: Good for beginners. (*Self to Outer Self; Energy; Phrasing;* unit 9, *Social Behavior*)

Other Applicable Improvs (for page numbers see index)
Trust Circle
Relax by Half
Tension Plop
The Cloud
Tension Release Walk
Lifting
Twist to Whirl
Balance
Carry Yourself
Right/Left Discrimination
Supports
Rigid
Weights
Three Punches
Toss

Improv Ideas
roll and jump
inside outside upside down
turn on the window ledge
rubber band
whirling dervish
free fall
moving fast, yet balanced
with the left
up/down/side

Touch

Our sense of touch has two aspects: we can either touch or be touched. When we touch ourselves, both aspects are activated. Investigate this sense as both instigator and recipient.

A Type of Touch
Alone, on your own body, explore different kinds of touch: poking, scratching, stroking, slapping. Respond with movement. Try to split your perception and attend only to the sensation of being touched, or only to the texture of the surface you are touching (e.g., hair, facial skin, fingernails). Do as a duet, alternating roles of toucher and touchee with your partner. Use many different body parts to touch with. Note: This improv helps ease improvisers into touching and being touched by people with whom they do not have a personal or intimate relationship. Interpersonal touch is a fundamental aspect of the improv experience, and this particular structure approaches it in a simple, straightforward fashion. *(Self to Important Other; Movement and Movement Qualities)*

Body Contours
Explore the contours of your own body. What is rounded, pointy, thick, hard, or concave? Translate the contours into movement. *(Self to Outer Self; Space)*

Freeze Duet
Toucher freezes different body parts of his moving partner, who keeps as many other parts "alive" as possible until they're deadened by the freeze. A double tap can unfreeze a part. *(Self to Important Other)*

As Clay
In pairs. One person is the sculptor, the other is the clay. Sculptor forms the clay into different designs. Clay can be passive, receptive, or can resist. When sculptors are finished have them look at the other pieces of sculpture which were created. Review their own and then add themselves on as an integral part of the sculpture. Limitation 1: Use any body part other than hands. Limitation 2: Use no direct touch. (If they are stymied, propose using breath, sound, or fanning in place of direct touch.) Note: Good for beginners. *(Self to Outer Self; Self to Important Other; unit 8, Art Forms)*

Touch to Learn
Leader brings in different types of objects of varying size, shape,
weight, and texture that would be interesting to explore via touch.
Movers explore the object with eyes closed and then move the
way it feels (e.g., long slow curves, small and heavy, prickly, a
rolling sphere). The goal is sensitization, not identification.

Other Applicable Improvs (for page numbers see index)
Back-to-Back
Blind Milling

Improv Ideas
bumping
cactus fluff
pick pat poke
destroy
fingertips on your back
don't touch!
shattered or shattering glass
creepy crawlers

Sight

Improvs oriented toward this sense can accentuate either vision or
its absence.

Picture Pose
(Preparation: A Position) Leader or movers bring in pictures of
people (sports or news photos, cartoons, advertisements). All
are laid out on the floor. Choose three pictures and label them
1, 2, 3. They become, in that order, the beginning, middle, and
ending shapes of an improv. Begin in shape 1; move according
to its edict, knowing that it must eventually bring you to the
second shape, and that one to the third. Hold each shape three to
five seconds. Shuffle the order and repeat. Note: Particularly
useful for people who have difficulty holding endings. Good
for kids. (*Self to Outer Self; Space; Transitions;* unit 8, *Art
Forms*)

Total Darkness
Completely darken the room. How do you move in total darkness? How could your dance be known to a spectator? Introduce single tiny light, such as a pen flashlight. What changes? Note: Good for the externally oriented mirror-gazers because it emphasizes the kinesthetics rather than the visuals of movement. (Unit 7, *Theatrics*)

Flashlight
In twos. Darken the room. Each pair has a flashlight. One person shines the light on the other's body and only that part of the body may move. Use only those parts that (1) are presently lit, or (2) have been lit, until the whole body is moving. Change roles. (Unit 7, *Theatrics*)

Mural
"Paint" a mural on an imaginary wall (or a real one) using body parts as a paint brush. Consider the color and texture, the line and shape, and where you get the paint from and how you get and apply it. Note: A winner with children. (Unit 8, *Art Forms*)

Dictated Conversation   See chapter 9, "Advanced Challenges." (Unit 9, *Social Behavior*)

Other Applicable Improvs (for page numbers see index)
Mirroring
Blind Milling
Shadows
Progressive Sculpture
Progressive Mural
Room as Movement Score
Nonsound Accompaniment
Sound/Nonsound Accompaniment
Lights
Figurative Sculpture
Abstract Paintings

Improv Ideas
instant design
zero in
blue on blue
peripheral vision
soft focus
eye contact
a field of yellow

Hearing

These improvs cultivate the skill of paying attention to what you hear—receptive responsive listening.

The Big Hum

Everyone lying down together; eyes closed. They all begin to drone the first syllable of their names: They drone until they're out of breath, and immediately start again. It begins quietly, then may increase in volume. First simply listen to the concert. Once the sound is established begin moving. (*Self as Part of the Group; unit 6, Accompaniment*)

The Paragraph

The leader reads a nonnarrative paragraph or sentence; as the leader reads, respond to the tempo, rhythm, and phrasing of the words, not to their sense. Reread it with a different emphasis, intonation, intention, volume, and pitch. Also try making up and using nonsense vocalizations ("Asquire sen toff, sa min, sa hoff"). (*Time; unit 6, Accompaniment; unit 8, Art Forms*)

Rhythmic Phrase

Sitting in a circle facing in, take turns patting, pounding, and snapping out a short, simple, rhythmic phrase. One person does a phrase and the rest of the group repeats it twice. Proceed around the circle until everyone has contributed one phrase. Begin again with three or four repeats of each rhythmic unit; this time respond with body in movement instead of sound. (*Time; Phrasing; unit 6, Accompaniment*)

Pick an Instrument
The leader plays any piece of music. Movers choose one instrument they hear in the piece and respond to it only, trying to embody its rhythm, tone, melody, and so on. (Unit 6, *Accompaniment*)

Other Applicable Improvs (for page numbers see index)
Blind Milling (with body sounds for signals)
Pair Walk (with body sounds for signals)
Progressive Sound
Prepared Piano and Created Instruments
Becoming
Mickey Mouse the Music
Leader's Voice
Self-Accompaniment
Poems (leader recites poem during the improv; could manipulate it as well)
Music
Mise-en-Scène

Improv Ideas
reverberations
percussive response
callings
word statue
jabberwocky
room noise
attacking, soothing, or disturbing sounds

Speech

It is quite usual for people who are at home in movement improv to freeze up when they're asked to work with sound. Improvs encouraging exploration of breath, vocalizing, and verbalizing add a vital dimension.

Breath
Experiment with the different sorts of sounds made with different types of breathing (hisses, snores, inhales, puppylike panting,

gasps, ugh-exhales). Begin with the sound only; then add movement. Note: Good for beginners.

Voice/Movement Conversation
Try having a conversation between your voice and your movement (movement asks, voice answers). Can also be done in pairs, alternating the movement and the spoken parts. Voice responses can be sensical or non-sensical, words or vocal sounds. (Self to Important Other; unit 6, *Accompaniment*)

Vocal Accompaniment
Working with any kind of movement, each person provides their own vocal accompaniment. Attend to tone, quality, duration, tempo, force, and pitch. Try for aural equivalent to the movement, and then for counterpoint. (Unit 6, *Accompaniment*)

Free Association
The leader calls out single words; everyone free-associates verbally. Then let it change to a movement response. Movement response initially can be brief but should gradually lengthen. (Unit 8, *Art Forms*)

Other Applicable Improvs (for page numbers see index)
Blind Milling (with vocalization)
Stomach Laugh
Progressive Sound
Phrase Shape
Name Chant
Poems (movers recite poem or part of it as they move; could manipulate it as well)

Improv Ideas
my name
child's verse
stuttering
it's all Greek to me
rapping
singing in the rain

Smell and Taste

Smell is considered the most primitive sense. It is often capable of instigating recall of long-forgotten and otherwise inaccessible instances in one's life. Taste, of which smell is an integral component, is furthermore so closely linked with hunger and survival that it thereby offers a variety of associated ideas.

Spices
Bring in spices and herbs in different envelopes. Free rein from there.

From the Past
Have individuals being in things with a smell or taste reminiscent of something in their past or something of particular significance to them. Pass them around. Improvise with their own and/or each other's.

New Tastes
Everyone brings in things to taste. The movement response may be to texture, flavor, or any reference they call to mind. Try this blindfolded and with the nose pinched closed so the sense of taste operates independently from the sense of smell and sight.

UNIT 4. ELEMENTS OF MOVEMENT
Space

Positive/Negative
First work with making shapes with your own body, attending to the overall design in space and the facings of different body parts. Shift your attention to the negative spaces. Move, paying attention to how the negative spaces change as a result of your movement. Keep moving and shift focus to positive; keep shifting. Note: A helpful reorientation for those constantly inclined to check out how they look. (Self to Outer Self; Self to Important Other)

Curved/Angular
Explore both design elements in terms of (1) the designs of your body, and (2) the paths in space. Try curved sustained movement

with spiraling and twisting; travel in large sweeping circles and tight little curls. Try angular, with abrupt changes of direction, locomotion in straight lines and sharp angles, sudden stops and starts. Mix curved and angular. Note: Good for beginners.

Direct/Indirect
First work with the notion of a single, direct, spatial focus. Then work with indirect: the simultaneous overlapping of multiple foci. From many different parts of your body attend to all the details in the entire space *at once*—the ceiling fan, a person moving behind you, the light switch, your heel. Mix the two types of focal attention. Note: This is based on Laban's Effort/Shape terminology.

Ceiling
Alternately choose different body parts to be imaginatively attached to tracks in the ceiling. Move with that restriction. Note: Good for beginners.

Planes
Work in each of the three planes: vertical (emphasize up and down, with side-to-side secondary, but no forward or backward); horizontal (emphasize side-to-side with forward or backward secondary, but no up or down); sagittal (emphasize forward and backward, with up and down secondary, but no side-to-side). Vertical is also known as the Door Plane, horizontal as the Table Plane, and sagittal as the Wheel Plane. These nicknames are useful for clarifying the delineations of the movement. (*Self to Outer Self*)

Change Perspective
Focus on doing an improv to be viewed from the ceiling, or from underground. Move only on the walls. Have half the group watch any regular improv upside down.

Facings
Work with your back always to an imaginary audience (with the left side, etc.). Note: This can be used to cultivate stage presence, the ability to project and for using unusual parts of the body as the main speaker.

Floor Patterns
People bring in designs for floor patterns. Move to your own, to someone else's. Variations can be structured in terms of facing (e.g., always face the left side of the room while you make a three-quarters circle clockwise and a diagonal to down right).

Elevation
While lying down, sitting, or bending over as you stand, explore different ways of jumping or getting as much of you off the floor as possible. *(Manipulation)*

Walk in Straight Lines   See chapter 5, "Leaders' Concerns."

The Wall   See chapter 5, "Leaders' Concerns." *(Self to the World)*

Getting Out I & II   See chapter 5, "Leaders' Concerns." (Unit 9, *Social Behavior*)

Other Applicable Improvs (for page numbers see index)
Blind Milling
Open-Close
Point Base
Shadows
Tiny Parts
Distortions
Kinespheres
Flight
Up/Down
Progressive Mural
Progressive Sculpture
Poison
Alone in the Studio
Still Shape
Body Contours
Picture Pose
Attached Below
A Position
Nonsound Accompaniment

Sound/Nonsound Accompaniment
Sets
Create an Environment
Figurative Sculpture
Abstract Paintings

Improv Ideas
corridors
part-of-body dance
levels
small to large
space warp
private dance
fractured space

Time

Fast/Slow
Work with fast, then slow. Alternate them and then try simultaneous counterpoint. Try accelerando and ritardando. Note: Good for beginners.

A Slice of Time
The leader beats out eight counts with an accent on count one, repeating the accompaniment as each person creates an eight-count phrase. Do the same phrase in four counts, then in two, then in one, speeding up the movement accordingly. Repeat again, each time getting slower, by going to sixteen counts then thirty-two. Now speed up and slow down within one repeat of the movement phrase. May be done according to clock time rather than drumbeat. Note: Composition oriented. (*Phrasing;* unit 6, *Accompaniment*)

Arrests and Interruptions
With or without music, use free movement with sudden and unexpected stoppages. This can be determined by the mover or the leader (the leader may push *pause* on the tape deck). Note: Can produce interesting phrasing shapes as well as variety in timing. (Unit 6, *Accompaniment*)

Meters
Work in different meters, the usual ones (3/4, 6/8, 4/4) and the
unusual ones (5/4, 7/8). The leader claps to establish the tempo
and metric pattern. For advanced work, mix meters. Note: Could
be oriented toward composition work. (Unit 6, *Accompaniment*)

Regular/Irregular
The leader establishes a regular beat (with or without a predictable accent) and the movers respond; then the leader (1) unex-
pectedly changes the regularity of the tempo; (2) puts in stops
and/or changes of accent; (3) maintains a regular beat while the
movers vary their movements in counterpoint to it. Note: This and
the preceding four improvs are good in a Music for Dance class.
(Unit 6, *Accompaniment*)

Stillness
Using any movement motivation (e.g., explore traveling, turns, and
levels), find places of stillness. Vary the length of the stillness.
Pay attention to *the way you are still* and to the beginning and
ending of the still time (e.g., there can be abrupt stops or gradual
changes into or out of a stillness).

Other Applicable Improvs (for page numbers see index)
Breathing
Progressive Sound
The Paragraph
Rhythmic Phrase
Self-Accompaniment

Improv Ideas
the going
pauses
hurry up and wait
melt time; splinter a second
Waltzing Matilda
time warp
déjà vu

Energy

Explosive Movement
Work with explosive movement. Vary the size and length of the
explosion, the body part, the follow through, and so on. Do it
alone, in twos, in groups. *(Movement and Movement Qualities)*

Pushing
Push something light, something heavy, something prickly, something sticky. Be pushed (with consent or with resistance). Push
something immovable. Work in pairs or small groups with the
same idea.

Rigid
Find the possibilities for movement with a rigid body; explore
various dramatic contexts and connotations. Mix in times of being
jelly-jointed, for relief or contrast. Do alone, then with a partner.
(Kinesthesia)

Sustained/Percussive
Work with each type of movement independently, and then
alternate. Try simultaneously with different parts of the body.

Weights
Work with real or imagined weights on various places on the
body. Move them; throw them; their sizes and shapes can vary.
Note: The passive use of rounded, heavy, smooth objects will
orient this toward relaxation. *(Kinesthesia)*

Gongs and Crystals
Imagine you are surrounded by huge suspended cymbals and
gongs. Use the different parts of your body to play them. Vary the
ways in which you hit them. Work with the reverberations and
the volume of the sound produced. Do the same with the finest
tiny crystal bells. Alternate between the two. Note: Good for
beginners.

Three Punches
Using different parts of your body as the source of the impulse,

experiment with three kinds of punches: (1) with a follow-through; (2) with a rebound; and (3) stopped dead. Mix. *(Kinesthesia)*

Away from Lyric   See chapter 5, "Leaders' Concerns."

Other Applicable Improvs (for page numbers see index)
Twist to Whirl
Explosions
Impulse/Follow-through
Suspend, Fall, and Recovery
The Surge
Hurricane

Improv Ideas
comet
puppets
moon walk
collapse
the impossible lift
weak/strong
uptight/indulgence

Movement and Movement Qualities

Move!
Exploration of any single type of movement or movement quality, such as jump, shake, turn, slide, twist, melt, fall, run, tap, bend, crawl, jitter, swing, slither, thrust, hop, zap, squirm, stretch, strut, stagger, throw, pounce. Note: Good for beginners.

Images
Explore any images high in movement stimulation: fireflies, chewing gum, blizzard, cheese fondue, cherry bomb, wilted, frolic, drudgery, hot pepper, lightning, typewriter.

Locomotor Patterns
Give a sequence of repeatable locomotor skills (three hops, a fall, two rolls to standing, a jump, and four runs). Vary the way the movements are done (changing the timing, amount of space cov-

ered, etc.) but not the order. Note: With beginners, allow time for improvisation with each locomotor skill separately before stringing them together. Then put two or three together before going on to the full sequence of five or more. (Manipulation)

Tasks
A variety of tasks and gestures is called out at random; movers must go immediately, without transition, from one to another (put on suntan lotion, hang up the laundry, hitch a ride, pick up spilt M&Ms). In the beginning allow time between the tasks, then speed up. Note: Some postmodern choreographers create interesting works based on this random and nonlinear progression of ordinary movement. (Unit 7, Theatrics; unit 8, Art Forms)

Toss
In twos. Move with a specific movement quality; then toss it to your partner. He catches and plays with it, maintaining the quality but changing the movement; then he tosses it back. Gradually let the quality change as it gets tossed, caught, and manipulated. (Self to Important Other; Self as Part of the Group; Kinesthesia; Manipulation)

Changing
In a circle everyone starts with the same movement quality, given by the leader. One person comes to center and offers a development; the group adopts the change in quality (but does not copy the specific movement). Once the new quality is established, that person leaves; another takes the center and changes it again.

Attached Below
Walk any path through the space. There are thick elastics attached to different parts of your body which connect to tracks below the ground. You are free to continue to move through space yet are limited and controlled by the constant yet flexible attachments. The places on your body that the elastics are attached to should change, first an elbow, then a knee and head, for example. Include going to the floor but don't stay there; keep traveling. (Space)

Exploration
This improv deliberately mixes components of movement instead
of isolating one out for extensive exploration. It is about change.
It can be done with various aspects of movement; try different
combinations. Here are the instructions for one set. Start in a
circle, facing in, eyes closed. Do the **Mid-Brain Warm-up** (in
chapter 5, "Leaders' Concerns"). "Keeping the easy flow, move
faster; even faster, but keep the flow continuous. Keep it going
until you have to slow down, to about medium speed. Keep the
easy flow and make all the movement very small, keeping it tight
around your body; try different parts of your body—elbows, hips.
Staying as fast as you can, let the movement get bigger; even
bigger so you can travel and leap. Let it slow down a little but
keep the movement large and start gathering the space around
you; bring it in. Let the movement be any speed, any size, but find
different ways to gather the space. Gather with your chin, the
inside of your leg, your head and knees. Vary the size of what you
are gathering and your attitude toward it. What you are gathering
starts to give you resistance, so you have to work to get it; add
energy, strength, tension." Note: It is good for beginners but certainly can work as a warm-up or as a preparation for advanced
complex improvs, introducing concepts.

Other Applicable Improvs (for page numbers see index)
Twist to Whirl
Right/Left Discrimination
Human Evolution
Becoming Civilized
Flight
Explosions
Imaginary Environment
A Type of Touch
Explosive Movement
Alien Link
Stacking
Air/Earth/Fire/Water
The Sixties
Days of Knights and Ladies

Improv Ideas
sports (everything from wrestling to water ballet)
Laban's Effort Cube (float, punch, glide, slash, dab, wring, flick,
    press)
frenzy
fury
constantly accommodating
potatoes on a full moon

Unit 5. Composition
Phrasing

The Surge
Start with **Mid-Brain Warm-up** (see chapter 5, "Leader's Concerns"). As you are moving, let there be surges of energy which
carry the movement for a while. Vary the length of the surges,
sometimes really stretching it out and at other times cutting it
short. Also vary the way the surge dissipates. Try letting the surge
start in different places in your body. Let some travel, take you
to the floor. Keep it active, moving. Note: Good for beginners.
(*Energy; Transitions; Manipulation*)

Phrase Shape
Use the shape of the following phrases rather than their literal
meanings. Do two or three different short improvs to each. (1) "I
whistled as I waited while I wanted just to scream; Aahhh!"
(2) Without warning, the bomb exploded, flinging fragments of
sound, memory, and chaos everywhere. In a moment, all was still.
(3) Climbing up, high, higher, highest, peak. Free fall, riding
down.
   Try any of these adding self-made sounds. For a more advanced
version, string the above together in any order to make one longer
unit. (Unit 6, *Accompaniment*)

Phrase Duration
Working with a variety of different isolated and combined parts of
the body, experiment with achieving phrases whose *duration*
approximates: a hiccup; the tickle preceding a sneeze; blowing up

a balloon, setting it free to float in the sky, losing sight of it; getting bumped off a trolley, picking yourself up, getting chased by a thief, crawling into a hiding place. Each successive phrase is a little longer. Note that the last one is actually an umbrella phrase comprised of four smaller ones.

Other Applicable Improvs (for page numbers see index)
Breathing
Suspend, Fall, and Recovery
Impulse/Follow-through
Rhythmic Phrase
A Slice of Time
Outer Silence/Inner Music

Improv Ideas
waves
thunder and lightning
up, down, and around; up, down, and...
around and around you go—each time higher, better, brighter
mixing phrase lengths
phrase shapes from abstract paintings

Overall Form

A Way to Go
Give the structure of an entire improv in graphic form:

(1)   (2)

Try it as a solo, trio, or using the whole group. Design more complex forms and try them. Note: See chapter 8, "Create Your Own Improv," for a discussion of ending at a high point.

Create a Score
Before class, each mover creates a movement score. (A movement score can be anything that generates and organizes movement for an improv.) Scores may be realized individually or collectively.

Half the fun is thinking up what kind of score it will be. See
Room as a Movement Score and **Picture Pose** as examples. Note:
Research the work of Earle Brown, John Cage, Merce Cunningham,
Anna Halprin, and Trisha Brown.

Chance
Divide the class into four groups. Group A does individual free
movement except that whenever they see the color green (a ribbon
or scarf worn by someone), they must turn in some way (this is
the only time turning is allowed; the duration is determined by
the turner). Each person in Group B chooses someone in Group A
whose movement they copy. Whenever their person turns, they
must freeze until circled and then find someone else (in Group A)
to copy. Group C are the musicians; they can make sounds with
their voices, bodies, instruments, or props; they work as a group
independent of the movers but whenever an individual in this
group sees two or more people frozen at the same time, he stops
playing, goes into the dance space, and finds some way of circling
around one of the frozen people before returning to the music
group to resume playing. Group D has a pack of cards with which
they play Go Fish. The person whose turn it is to "go fish" picks
up the green ribbon or scarf, does a series of turns and jumps
anywhere in the room, and then returns to continue the card
game. Note: Another triggering device can be used instead of the
card game.

Interruptions
The following may be layered over any fairly simple improv
structure. The leader determines a series of signals which will
interrupt or qualify the ongoing improv (e.g., when you hear a
whistle, go to the ground; if the lights blink, your movement
becomes quick, jerky).

Accumulations
As a solo, do one short movement, repeat it and add one new one,
repeat each and add another, and so on. Hints: Build sub-units so
that there is a kinesthetic logic uniting them; sing to yourself.
Have half the group watch.

Accumulations Minus One
As above but each time drop the first one, keeping only the last
three: 1; 1, 2; 1, 2, 3; 2, 3, 4; 3, 4, 5.... Make each addition
longer—a phrase rather than just a single movement. Include
traveling (this can make some movements place-specific and
therefore more memorable). Do as a duet. Note: This and the
previous improv could work well for performance. *(Self to
Important Other)*

Given
Set the first and last movement phrases; improvise the passage in
between. This could work with any size group—solo, duet, and so
on. It could also be used as a performance piece, especially with two
simultaneous duets using the same given movements. *(Transitions)*

Reduction   See chapter 9, "Advanced Challenges."

Journey   See "Special Populations," for the basic improv; then
see the rest of the chapter for adaptations for various populations.
(Self to the World)

    Other Applicable Improvs (for page numbers see index)
    Breathing (after becoming comfortable with the breath's internal
        phrasing, repeat and pay attention to how they accumulate to
        an overall form)
    Together
    Order—Chaos—Order (may result in ABA or ABC form)
    Rhythm Circle
    Multiple Focus (with an eye to overall form)
    Outer Silence/Inner Music

    Improv Ideas
    building/decaying
    a-b-a
    canon
    rondo
    a narrative
    a double narrative merges

Transitions

Two Sides of the Room
The leader assigns a specific movement aspect for each side of the room (e.g., left—fast/sustained, right—slow/abrupt; or left—big, right—little). They need not be opposites (left—a sad clown; right—weak/low level) and you could posit some relating on one side (circle someone). Find different ways of changing from one side to the other, over and over again.

Alien Link
Pick any two movement aspects. Move from one to another, always using a third, unrelated movement as a transition. Go back and forth a number of times. The first time you do this improv use only one kind of link (shaking). Then try it again using a variety, but be sure to keep them alien to the two given aspects. *(Movement and Movement Qualities)*

Passing By
The leader gives a sequence of four different types of movement (e.g., rolls, twists, falls, runs). The transition from one to the other has to be by way of an interaction with another person(s). *(Self to Important Other)*

A Position
Given: a position. Find five ways to get into it; five ways to get out. In a series of one-minute improvs, use the position as (1) an ending, (2) a beginning, (3) a way-station. *(Self to Outer Self; Space)*

Repetition
Begin with any simple movement and keep repeating it until it mutates into another movement. Then do the same with that movement. Do not allow yourself to decide the change; they are slow in coming. Have the patience to allow it to find its organic transformation.

Slow Changes
In a circle, do the preceding improv as a group. One person starts and everyone follows; once the change occurs, the person on his

right makes the next change and so on, around the circle. Emphasize staying with the movement repetition as long as it takes to make the kinesthetically motivated transition to the next movement, distinguishing these from transitions that are mentally determined. Note: The leader can reject any unauthentic transformation, in which case the improviser tries again. After a while, the movers can also reject an inorganic transition. (*Self as Part of the Group;* unit 9, *Social Behavior*)

Version 1. Person doing the initial movement and transition is in the center of the circle and gives the new movement to someone in the circle who brings it to the center and transforms it. Others in the circle can either move with the person in the center or not, but they must remain ready to take on the movement at any time.

Version 2. As above, but with facial expressions added.

Version 3. As above, but with accompanying sounds added. Note: Since facial expression and sounds add a significant dramatic component, these variations can become very powerful. (*Accompaniment*)

Version 4. As above, but start expanding involvement geometrically, with each person giving the new movement (facial expression and sound) to two other people who then make a transformation and pass it on to two more. Once everyone has become active, allow the improv to proceed in its own direction.

Other Applicable Improvs (for page numbers see index)
Suspend, Fall, and Recovery
Human Evolution (focus on transitions rather than on each
    stage)
Roar In
Picture Pose
Rhythmic Phrase
The Surge
Given
Three Kinds of Movement
A Goddess or a God

Improv Ideas
abrupt about face
he slowly came around
indecision
unknown crossings
thrown into the next
over the crest
around the corners
partings
quick reversals

Manipulation

These are ways of manipulating the physical properties of movement. The goal is simply to develop skill in enriching movement, allowing the mover to stay with and develop a movement instead of wandering from one idea to another. Manipulation thus maintains internal integrity while expanding and developing organic form; it lets the improv be about itself. For an improviser it is a fundamental and teachable skill. The following is the preparation for every improv in this section. The leader creates a short movement motif (e.g., draw an arc with the arm, ending with closing the fist; uncurl the body then shake the head). It should be quite simple; the complexities will come later. Repeat the motif, trying each of the following manipulations. Keep each change pure, changing only the aspect called for (don't let smaller become faster).

1. Repetition. Repeat exactly the same

2. Retrograde. Perform it backward. Start at the end and follow it back through space—like a movie run backward.

3. Inversion: upside-down (∩ becomes ∪) or lateral (Γ becomes ⅂). For upside-down inversion, you may have to lie on the floor or stand on your head. (This can be tricky and often impossible, but don't dismiss it on those grounds.)

4. Size: condense/expand. Take the motif and do it as small as you can. Try it even smaller. Now take the movement and make it bigger, as big as you can.

5. Tempo: fast/slow/stop. Take the motif and do it faster, now as fast as possible. Keep it the same size. Do it as slowly as you can. Find places for stillness in it. Try it with different length stillnesses.

Each time you try it put the stillness in different places. Mix: fast, slow, and various stillnesses.

6. Rhythm. Vary the rhythm but not the tempo. The variety and pattern of the beats should be altered, not the speed or the length of time it takes to accomplish. If, for example, the original rhythm was ♩ ♩, try doing it ♪ ♪ ♪ 𝄾.

7. Quality. Vary the movement quality. Try the same movement quivery, drifting, with erratic tension, and so on.

8. Instrumentation. Perform the movement with a different body part; try several different parts of the body. Trade your movement with someone else's. Have the whole group do it.

9. Force. Vary the amount of force you use in producing the movement. Do it with a great deal of strength, from beginning to end. Now repeat it again, with very little force, gently, weakly. Carefully try to keep the change in force only.

10. Background. Change the design of the rest of the body from its original position and repeat the motif. Let the rest of the body be doing something while the motif is going on. Sit instead of stand. Try perhaps twisting all the rest of you into a knot while still performing the regular motif. Add another person (maybe having them stand behind you and use their arms).

11. Staging. Perform the motif at a different place on the stage and/ or with a different facing or relation to other people or things in the improv. If it is moving through space, try making it travel in another direction (e.g., sideways or on a diagonal instead of backward).

12. Embellishment (ornamentation). The movement itself can have the embellishment (e.g., little loops or jigjags occurring along the path of the movement); or a part of the body can be embellished as it is involved in the movement (as the arm moves, wiggle the fingers or make a fist); or try embellishing both the body and the path of movement at the same time.

13. Change of planes/levels. Change the motif to a different plane: the horizontal, the vertical, the sagittal plane or any other slice of space. Do it on a different level. Trace the path of the gesture and use it as a floor pattern, move along that.

14. Additive/incorporative. Additive: While doing the original motif, simultaneously execute any kind of jump, turn, or locomotor pattern (triplet, run, slide). Incorporative: Make the original motif

into a jump, turn, or locomotor pattern. Although this can be tough or impossible with some motifs, approach it with a sense of "how can the original motif be jumped, turned, moved from place to place?" A series of chassés would be an example of the way an arc could be realized as a locomotor pattern.

15. Fragmentation. Use only a part of the motif, any part. Consider it as an entity in itself, use it to attend to a detail, a part worth isolating that might otherwise be overlooked. Or use several parts of it, such as the beginning third, a tiny piece halfway through, or the very end to create a new movement.

16. Combination. Combine any of the above so that they happen at the same time. This lets you combine affinities (faster with smaller) or antagonists (faster with larger). Combine three or four manipulations (fragmentation/inversion/embellishment, or inversion/retrograde/slower/different background). *This is where the really interesting possibilities emerge.* Variety and complexity grows as you combine more and more manipulations.

Mixing the Manipulations

"Using the same motif play with combining a number of manipulations as you improvise. Use any of the motif manipulations as they occur to you. As you move I will call out some suggestions. If you can use the suggestion at the time, fine; if not, ignore it and continue with what you are doing." Repeat again with half the group watching. Have them note the variety of ways the motif is developed but, more importantly, how it is united by the common bond of a shared motif. Repeat again with everyone creating their own motif. Note: This is important work for beginners. At first the movers may be timid of this improv; it seems so complex and precise. It would reassure them if you could explain the following. "As you improvise, these isolated categories will come together without you having to pick or choose. You may decide to make it bigger and as you do so, it will get slower, the plane will change, the background will accommodate, or ornaments grow. Possibly an intention will suggest itself and dictate the next set of manipulations. Soon you will get involved and forget to consciously dictate the changes; they will come and take over, one change rushing in with its own demands, with a

fancy step for traveling, or with a bound into a jump. This kind
of mixing and mushing various possibilities is the ultimate aim
of the skill of manipulation, allowing you to be imaginatively
explorative."

As One
Create a motif for two people. The movement can start on one
person and finish on the other; or two people can be so inter-
twined that the movement automatically includes both of them; or
one may support the other so that the movement is impossible
alone. Or you can simply use any movement motif and develop it
as a duet. The movement must be *very short*, ending so it can be
repeated without adjustments. Start by simply repeating the motif
a number of times, then let it develop, not only in terms of
movement but in relation to your partner. At first each mover
should only use her own material but later she should consider
the entire motif (the movement of both people) as material to
develop; in other words you can use your partner's part of the
motif and mix it with yours. You may even completely switch
material. Note: The leader may want to insure that the beginning
motifs are sufficiently succinct. *(Self to Important Other)*

As Three or Thirteen
Create a motif and develop it as a group. Note: Advanced work.

Stacking
Instead of using a specific movement as a motif, use a movement
concept. It helps to start with a specific example such as, in this
case, sitting on the floor and stacking one ankle above the other.
Stack other parts of the body; stack while turning, unstack, and so
on. *(Movement and Movement Qualities)*

Favorite Movement
Identify a movement that seems to crop up often in your dancing;
manipulate it. Note: This is for people who have been moving
long enough to be able to identify their personal stylistic gestures.
(See chapter 9, "Advanced Challenges.")

Other Applicable Improvs (for page numbers see index)
Sun Worship
Elevation
Locomotor Patterns
Toss
The Surge

Improv Ideas
manipulation of a game (hopscotch, football),
             a movement quality,
             a type of movement (turn, lunge, fall),
             a routine (eating, combing hair),
             a gesture,
             a prop,
             someone else

Abstraction

A helpful preparation for this entire section is the preceding one (Manipulations.) You may also want to review the section on abstraction and the abstract in chapter 2, "The Experiential Body of Knowledge." For the pure abstract, use improvs concerned exclusively with the medium of movement (see unit on Elements of Movement).

Also try the following. Have each person come up with as long a list as possible of *nonstandard uses* for any single commonplace object (such as a funnel, wheel, brick). Everyone works on the same object. Lists are brought in and read. Responses which make use of radical changes in the normal size, composition, or location of the object indicate more abstract or lateral thinking.

Line

(Preparation: **Room as Movement Score**) This improv is composed of a series of very curt directives. Each is given independently. It may be repeated, but under no circumstances should any additional information be given. After each instruction, the leader allows work to progress on it for a few minutes; then the next is given, and so forth. The improv takes approximately half an hour, and works very well for sizeable groups. Clarify, before beginning, that the movers are to respond as best they can to the instructions, as no additional information will be given. Also stress that no talking is allowed. Note: The early instructions will probably yield some befuddlement and not much creativity. Stay with it. This will change. Observe especially the difference in response between the last "Make a line" and the first. The instructions are:

Make a line.
Form a line.
Line up.
Line down.
Time-line
Lines.
Hotline.
Plumb line.
On the line.
Firing line.
L-I-N-E (spell out).
Curved lines.
Straight lines.
Broken line.
Out of line.
In line.
Make a line.

Discuss how this improv relates to creativity; to brainstorming; to the act of improvisation; to human social behavior. (*Self as Part of the Group*; unit 9, *Social Behavior*)

Hurricane
Work with the different movement aspects of a storm: the lashing winds, pounding surf, objects floating on the flood waters, the calm at the eye of the hurricane, the spiraling tornadoes that it spawns. (*Energy*)

Three Kinds of Movement
Consider three essentially different kinds of movement: a meaningful gesture (signaling a waiter); pure movement (leg moving from front to back in three counts); a task which actually accomplishes something (picking off lint).

Start with the gesture, manipulating it while staying with the original intent. For example, if the gesture is listening with hand to ear, you can allow your hip or ankle to be the ear and vary whom you are listening to—a timid child or an annoying pest. After you work with the gesture for a while let it become more abstract until the intent slips away and you are working with pure movement only. Then let the pure movement find a task into which it merges organically. You do not guide it there, or know what task it will become, but suddenly become aware that the movement has made that transformation. The trick is to be a detective, to keep an eye out for a clue for a movement that will lead to a task (broad scattering movements—picking off lint). Note: For experienced movers. An extension of this improv is to work only with gestures or tasks and have them continually transform from one to another. (*Transitions*; unit 9, *Social Behavior*; also see the discussion of objective/subjective in chapter 5, "Leaders' Concerns.")

An Object
Choose an item to work with: sticks, piano bench, rope, article of clothing. Explore as many ways as possible to be inspired by, use, or adapt that article in movement. Note: A fairly predictable progression from literal to abstract will occur as the improv is allowed to continue. (*Symbols*; unit 7, *Theatrics*)

The Movement Behind Using Props
(Preparation: **An Object**) Each person brings in one large item (table cloth, tree trunk, pillow) and a large quantity of a small item (yards of twine, 100 paper plates). Half of the group sets the space with the items. They watch while the other half improvises with the materials. Allow ten minutes for development. Stop the improv and ask everyone to repeat any two minutes without props and without the interaction of others. Repeat again in slow motion but with bursts of speed or unexpected stillnesses. Try again manipulating the use of space and energy. (Unit 7, *Theatrics*)

Sun Worship I
Start with everyone doing the Sun Worship ritual in unison. (You

can create your own or use the established Yoga version.) After a
number of repetitions begin to manipulate it: include some stillness, stretch out one part and skip another, change facings, or
background, run during some parts, turn at others, ornament,
repeat fragments, and so on. *(Manipulation)*

Sun Worship II
The sun can be seen as the symbol of the hero or the divine eye; it
is the source of warmth, light, renewal. Start with everyone doing the Sun Worship ritual (same as above) in unison. Keeping a
strong awareness of its symbolic connotations allow it to develop
as a shared activity *(Self as Part of the Group; Symbols)*. Note:
The preceding version approached the improv as an exercise in
movement abstraction. This version focuses attention on the unifying aspect of ritual and the symbolism of the sun.

Synesthesia
(*Synesthesia* is the transfer of an image to a sense other than the
one stimulated, as in "seeing" a sound.) Begin with input from
any of the senses, and transform your response to it via one of
the other senses. How does the smell of a rose look? What is the
shape of soft? How fast, and with what rhythms does the color
purple move? Note: You may want to precede this with work on
the senses individually. See unit 3, *Sensory Awakening*. For
experienced movers.

Other Applicable Improvs (for page numbers see index)
Name
Explore a Chair
Room as Movement Score
Transformation
Multiples
Masks
Poems
Abstract Paintings
Periods of Art
Plays and Scenes from Literature
A Goddess or a God

Improv Ideas
lines and spaces
shapes
Morse code
Mondrian's trees
Picasso's *Guitar Player*
Debussy's *La Mer*
the works of Alwin Nikolais, George Balanchine, or
    Merce Cunningham

Symbols

A symbol is something that stands for something else by association, resemblance, or convention. A material object frequently represents an abstract concept. Although some symbols have roots in the universal experience of mankind, their interpretation is ultimately personal and culture-bound.

The Fool

The Fool corresponds to the irrational, to blind impulse, and the unconscious. By acting mad and doing things which are ordinarily taboo, the Fool challenges the prevailing order. The Fool can also serve as a scapegoat. Work with any of these ideas improvisationally, alone or with others. (Unit 9, *Social Behavior*)

One Symbol, Three Approaches

Have each mover make a list of symbols, including some that are personally important. Where appropriate, use the graphic equivalent (e.g., 卍, ⊕, ♐, ♀). Pick one and view it (1) in terms of its design, timing, spatial, and movement connotations; (2) with regard to its history or ideational significance; and (3) for its emotional impact and overtones. Each mover improvises to her own selected symbol three separate times, using the three different references as the point of departure. Try improvising once more, letting the three aspects work together. Note: For experienced movers. (Unit 9, *Social Behavior*)

Monsters

Monsters symbolize a cosmic force only once removed from chaos.

Gradually distort your body to horrific proportions. Feel the monster growing inside of you, born of some ugly thought or feeling you have actually experienced. Allow it to take control. Note: Not for the easily impressionable or psychologically weak or disturbed. Be careful to provide a guided exit and return back to normal. (Unit 9, *Social Behavior*)

Air/Earth/Fire/Water
Use movement characteristics, and pertinent myths (South American, Greek, Navajo) to develop improvs about any of these elements *(Movement and Movement Qualities)*

Other Applicable Improvs (for page numbers see index)
Rhythm Circle
An Object
Sun Worship II
Symbolic Costumes
A Goddess or a God
Masculine/Feminine
Adult/Child

Improv Ideas
serpent
star spangled banner
acrobat (inversion or reversal)
shadow
mandala
antithetical symbols (flowers at a burial, skeleton at a feast)
hammer and sickle
white flag of surrender
the color white (red or black)

Unit 6. Accompaniment

Mickey Mouse the Music
Parallel the music with movement. Try again, but follow only one specific element (e.g., only the voice or sax). (*Hearing*; unit 8, *Art Forms*)

Stubborn/Accommodating
Bring in several different pieces of music. Begin with everyone having a few phrases of set movement. For each piece, people work with their set movements—first cling to the movement in its original mode, then allow it to become affected by the music. Note: This is useful for Theme and Variation, a basic compositional structure.

Outer Silence/Inner Music
People choose some music to sing to themselves as they move. The leader may specify a category from which they select their inner music; it may be stylistic (e.g., pop tunes, classical, city sounds), or qualitative (e.g., fast with great surges of power, or sparse). (Phrasing; Overall Form)

Leader's Voice
The leader provides a range of vocalizations, grunts, squeaks, hisses, gargles. They may be random or grouped into phrases, which may or may not be repeated. Movers respond in canon with movement (and sounds if desired). (Hearing)

Self-Accompaniment
Play with movement that calls for snaps, claps, stomps, and any kind of nonvocal sound created by the mover. Pay attention to the sounds' use for providing (1) continuous tempo; (2) accents; or (3) build-up or release of excitement. Note: Helpful in breaking balletic habits. (Hearing; Time)

Prepared Piano and Created Instruments
Use of regular instruments in nonordinary ways, or of noninstruments to create sounds. Divide class in half; half functions as orchestra, the other half as dancers. (Hearing)

Machine Make-a-Sound
With the whole group watching, one person begins a simple, repetitive movement and accompanying sound; one at a time, the rest add on. Note: Fun for children.

Name Chant

All stand in a circle, shoulder to shoulder, except for one person who is in the center with hands at his sides and eyes closed. He needs to stay straight, but not rigid. Put one hand on the person in the center and have the other hand on your neighbor. Chant the center person's name. Sway as you chant. The person in the center does not respond; he allows the others to move him. Verbally play with the name, making full use of the syllables, intonation, volume, and pitch. As each person takes a turn in the center you may want to add the options below. (Self as Part of the Group; Speech)

1. Be conscious of the natural phrasing and the way the movers work off each other, responding and playing. Allow counterpoint, harmonies, and so forth.

2. Allow other sounds to come in, nonsense sounds to compliment or counter. Build a rich sound texture, but the focus of the group is still the person's name.

3. Occasionally add real words or sentences.

4. Actor's option: Using characters from a play, start with the person's actual name, then switch to the character's name. Have the group's tone reflect the cast's attitude toward the character. Use some lines from the text.

Nonsound Accompaniment

Consider other types of accompaniment: blinking lights, fans and streamers, a parade of candles. Design your nonsound accompaniment and your relation to it (instigator, victim, partner, background). Improvise. (Sight; Space; unit 7, Theatrics)

Sound/Nonsound Accompaniment

Consider combinations: wind and thirty oversized rolling beach balls; bells and falling and rising balloons; rolling and falling hoops, a waterfall. (Sight; Space; unit 7, Theatrics)

Becoming   See chapter 7, "Music." (Hearing)

Other Applicable Improvs (for page numbers see index)
Stomach Laugh

Breathing
Progressive Sound
Rhythm Circle
The Paragraph
Rhythmic Phrase
The Big Hum
Pick an Instrument (using live musicians)
Voice/Movement Conversation
Vocal Accompaniment
A Slice of Time
Arrests and Interruptions
Meters
Regular/Irregular
Phrase Shape
Slow Changes Version III
In the Spirit but Without the Steps
Rodeo

Improv Ideas
animal voices
symbolic sounds
room sounds
wailing
laughing-giggling-gurgling
. . — (dot, dot, dash)
snow falling
a passing train
an avalanche

Unit 7. Theatrics

Sets
Use ladders, doors, windowsills, platforms, benches, barres, steps, door frames (all often found in a studio or backstage) as a set. Create a physical world, with hiding and soaring places. This improv may be split, so half the group creates the space for the other half. Note: Great for children—of all ages. (Self to the World; Space)

In Costume
Everyone comes in costume. Explore the options it opens and the restrictions it causes. Trade costumes or exchange parts to create new costumes. Try ones that have a built-in physical restriction (e.g., a straightjacket, roller skates).

Lights
Have a lighting designer work with the group onstage. She sets the lighting; the improvisers enter and move so as to take advantage of its possibilities. She throws cues, they respond. She may want to give a title, goal, intention, restriction, or other instructions. (Sight)

Cloth
Use large cloths as body covering, symbolic space, shelter.

Create an Environment
Lace the place with tape, elastic, plastic wrap, string, balloons. Note: For movers with some basic experience. (Self to the World; Space)

Transformation
The leader provides some props, costumes, sets. Improvisers use props as costumes, costumes as sets, and so on. Or use your body or another's as prop, set, or costume. (Abstraction)

Multiples
The studio is filled with duplicates of an object (chairs, ropes, scarves, or sticks). What are the added opportunities of having more (possibly even many more) than one of an object to work with? (Abstraction)

Symbolic Costumes
Work with a crown, a clerical collar, a black leather jacket. Try working both with, and counter to, the appropriate inferences. (Symbols; unit 9, Social Behavior)

Masks
See chapter 9, "Advanced Challenges." (*Abstraction*, unit 9, *Social Behavior*)

Video/Dance   See chapter 9, "Advanced Challenges."

Other Applicable Improvs (for page numbers see index)
Shadows
Elephant Game
Explore a Chair
Multimedia
Flashlight
Total Darkness
Tasks (with objects)
An Object
The Movement Behind Using Props
Nonsound Accompaniment
Sound/Nonsound Accompaniment

Improv Ideas
pools of light
ladders
makeup (old age, surrealistic, clown)
lampshades
swings
places to hide
in-the-round
guerrilla theater
umbrellas
duet with a candle

Unit 8. Art Forms

All art forms work with abstraction, form, style, and intent, but the unique essence of each derives from its medium (e.g., musical notes) and cannot readily be captured in another medium. Nevertheless many facets of one art can be used as stimuli for another. In this section we have provided some starting points for translating a given art form into movement. It is up to you, as leader, to make this material (in its style, form, subject, or medium) movement-specific and accessible. The more familiar someone (either the leader-creator of the improv, or the mover) is with the specific medium and the particular work of art, the simpler it will be to make the translation. Depending on the amount of movement information you provide, some of the following improvs might be better suited for your more experienced movers. But for the less experienced you may consider introducing the material in a series of improvs beginning with some that are rooted in movement aspects, such as **A Position** as preparation for **Photography** or **Figurative Sculpture.** (Actually many of the improvs already given may be good preparations for ones in this category. Look through them with that in mind.) Of course there are times when even beginners make an immediate intuitive jump, when there is no need for preparation. They just know how, for instance, to physically interpret Gertrude Stein's "a rose is a rose is a rose." A lot will depend on their own affinities, passions, and knowledge. For more ideas on using different art forms see: the section on actors in chapter 12, "Specific Populations," chapter 7, "Music," and the improvs **Toward a New Jazz Style** and **Cultural Heritage.**

Photography
Present any book of great photography; allow people to pick some photograph and then improvise from it. May also be done in pairs or groups. Try using photographs with and without people. (*Self to Important Other; Self as Part of the Group*)

Abstract Paintings
Attend to shape, color, size, placement, and the visual relationships of the work. (*Sight; Space; Abstraction*)

Figurative Sculpture
Show photos of the work of such sculptors as Giacometti, Rodin, Michaelangelo, or Arp for motivation. (*Self to Outer Self; Sight; Space*)

Films
Share images from films you've seen; choose one to work from (the timing of the chase in *The Keystone Cops*; the eating scene

in *Tom Jones*; the figure of death in *Amadeus*; 3CPO from Star Wars).

Realistic Art
Choose a realistic work of art in any medium. Try two different approaches: first, analyze and improvise to its compositional components (e.g., busy lines and cramped space), and second, improvise on the subject matter, message, or mood. Then mix the two approaches. How do they work together?

Periods of Art
Choose a period of art (Romantic, Impressionist, Cubist, Surrealist, Primitive, Baroque). Present examples, including art, architecture, fashion, music, theater, dance, literature, opera. Identify elements that you can work with in movement terms. Create an improv. (*Abstraction*)

Poems
Select a poem or a well-known adage ("The faster I run, the behinder I get") to use as the basis for an improv. Note: Watch out for overliteral treatment and adjust your instructions accordingly. (*Self to Outer Self; Self to the World; Hearing; Speech; Abstraction*)

Music
Consider using a piece of music for its image or idea rather than for its actual sound. Use Beethoven's *Eroica* Symphony, Mahler's *Kindertotenlieder*, or Mozart's *Requiem* for their powerful inspiration, or a popular song for its message and not for its beat. In other words, use the music as you would a painting. Improvise, without the music. When you are finished you might want to improvise to the music and compare the two improvs. (*Hearing*)

In the Spirit but Without the Steps
Try a "tango" or "waltz" to the music but without the established steps. Try it with no steps, rooted in one place or sitting or lying down. (Unit 6, *Accompaniment*)

Plays and Scenes from Literature
Choose a piece. Define it in terms of character, goal, action.
Translate into movement; create an improv. Try it again zeroing in
on a smaller aspect. *(Self as Part of the Group; Abstraction)*

Mise-en-Scène
(The setting of the scene.) Choose a setting (circus, city life, a war-
torn town, a lovers' reunion, the first snowfall). First improvise a
story dramatically in speech, with appropriate movement and
gestures. That sets the action. Then repeat the same scenario as
closely as possible without sound. Repeat again in slow motion.
Repeat again, fine tuning the movement: make the small movements smaller, the fast ones faster, and so on. This series is a
progression from literal, imitative work to a more abstract render-
ing of the same material. *(Self as Part of the Group; Hearing;
Abstraction)*

Dance Styles
Choose a style of movement, such as jazz, classical ballet,
Flamenco, or primitive. Identify the primary elements of that
idiom (e.g., for Flamenco—proud, high in the upper chest, spine
stern and erect; for primitive—grounded, pelvic strength and
mobility, sexual, low level, connection to the earth, use of
isolations, and emphasis on multirhythmic patterns). Investigate
the selected elements in improv. Note: See note for **Rodeo.**

Rodeo
Pick any established piece of choreography, such as Agnes
de Mille's *Rodeo*. Define it in any of a number of ways: by its
characters, story line, movement style, use of sets and props,
relation to music, mood, intent, thesis, and so on (hunchbacks in
Pilobolus's *Monkshead Farewell*, or the religious fervor of Doris
Humphrey's *Shakers*). Focus on one or two of these and create an
improv. Try this improv with and without the original music.
Note: Good multiple-use improv for dancers and choreographers.
With this improv and the one above **(Dance Styles)** we are only
considering the finished product of dance and not the process or
craft of choreography. (Unit 6, *Accompaniment)*

Dance Humor
Discuss things that make dance funny: plain funny movement, incongruous juxtaposition, exaggeration, illogical cause and effect, character, and so on. Create an improv. Note: Humor can't be forced. Look for humor in other improvs.[2]

The Sixties
Consider using city sounds, the music of John Cage, Gordon Mumma, or any taped speech, newscast, or trivial conversation as background. (Dancers may disregard the sound score, or not.) Look around and see ordinary everyday people doing what they do—driving a bus, waitressing, sawing wood, shaking out a dust mop, opening a door, rolling up some twine. Do those movements, pedestrian and mundane, one after another. Do functional things (scratching, adjusting your clothes). Intersperse tasks and functional movements with gestures (thumbing a ride, signaling "A-okay"), ordinary walking, lying down and rolling over, facial expressions. Sit on a chair, get up, sit down again, tap your fingers, throw a rock at a rat. Do these simply, naturally, purposefully. Interrupt a task with a jump or turn-around/walk-away; do a gesture with noncommittal aplomb, misfit a bored expression while doing hard manual labor. Do a series of unrelated pedestrian movements, tasks, gestures in nonordinary positions (run while lying down, type behind your back). Note: This draws from the postmodern emphasis on the validity of the natural actions of common people without affectations, technique, or elaboration. It democratizes space, time, and people. (*Movement and Movement Qualities*; unit 9, *Social Behavior*)

Other Applicable Improvs (for page numbers see index)
Postures
Progressive Mural
Progressive Sculpture
A Gift (with an actual art, ritual, or religious object)
Multimedia

[2]For ideas, see Lynne Anne Blom, "What Makes a Dance Funny?" *American Dance* 2, no. 1 (1986): 3–9.

As Clay
Mural
Picture Pose (using photography and painting)
The Paragraph (using famous lines)
Free Association (using titles of well-known art works)
Tasks
Slow Changes Version II
Mickey Mouse the Music
Masks
Other Cultures
Days of Knights and Ladies

Improv Ideas
Subjects
the good, the bad, and the ugly
the seven deadly sins
drama run backward
tales of terror
collage
the jitterbug
a mass
descent from the cross
bacchanal
landscape
a boy and his dog
coming home
a puzzle
a maze
the mystery
fairy tales
a portrait

Specific works
Walt Whitman, "I Sing America"
Norman Rockwell, *A Girl at the Mirror*
Andrew Wyeth, *Christina's World*
Anton Chekov, *The Seagull*
"A Train" (a jazz melody)

Frank Capa, "The Spanish Fighter at the Instant of Death '36" or
     "The Hill"
Charles Schulz, Snoopy
Jules Feiffer's cartoons
Walt Disney, *Fantasia*
Twyla Tharp, *Deuce Coupe*
Alwin Nikolais, *Tent*
Kurt Joss, *The Green Table*
Ingmar Bergman, *The Seventh Seal*
Phillip Glass, *Glassworks*
Igor Stravinsky, *Rite of Spring*
Martha Graham, *Clytemnestra*
Pina Bausch, *1980*
Martha Clarke, *Vienna: Lusthaus*
Antoine de St. Exupery, *The Little Prince*
Francisco José de Goya y Lucientes, *The 5th of May*

In the style of
James Joyce
Charlie Chaplin
Merce Cunningham
John Cage
Robert Raushenberg
Japanese Kabuki Theater
Les Ballets Trockadero de Monte Carlo
Henri Matisse
Georgia O'Keefe

Unit 9. Social Behavior

Hello/Good-bye
Try different ways of greeting and parting as the whole group mills
around the room. Note: Good for children. *(Self as Part of the
Group)*

Games
Games come from a need to move, to test skill (coordination and
strength), to plan and compete. They allow one to practice and

demonstrate certain skills while at the same time they involve rituals and luck. Games are often strongly social (team cooperation), with strict rules (thus raising the issue of cheating). They can be ritualistic and reflective of the world at large (e.g., chants originally being omens, curses, and protection rites). Create an improv using some of the many ideas associated with games. Note: Games such as tag, catch, leapfrog, and home-free offer possibilities that can be woven into the instructions of other improvs (especially if traces of them begin to appear in an ongoing improv). Delightful for children; good for all. *(Self as Part of the Group)*

A Goddess or a God
(Preparation: **Changing**)

Part 1. You are the medicine man or woman of your tribe, preparing to take on the power and knowledge of a specific deity in a sacred ritual. It can be the deity of war, love, peace, fertility, wine, destruction, flight, laughter. Establish your oneness with this deity through your movement; acquire its knowledge and thereby its power. Make the identity an integral part of your reflexes, your kinesthetic, emotional, and psychological systems. When the transfer of identity is solid, return to neutral.

Part 2. Form a circle and sway from side to side. One at a time, enter the circle and become your deity. The group, *as a tribe,* responds; they may worship, challenge, or take on the deity's characteristics. Note: For experienced movers. Could be useful and interesting to do some background work on rituals. Try it a second time with masks created by the movers. *(Self as Part of the Group; Abstraction; Symbols)*

Other Cultures
Select any motivational possibility from another culture (past or present), ethnic group, or region to use as a point of departure. This could include art, artifacts, social customs, rituals and religious practices, survival techniques, and so on. (Unit 8, *Art Forms*)

Masculine/Feminine
Exploration and turn-about of regular roles. First make a list of movement aspects that are stereotypically considered to be male

and female. Men explore the feminine list, women the masculine. Then try the appropriate roles. Now mix, being careful not to dilute. Try jumping abruptly from one to another as if in a conversation with two sides of yourself or between two different characters; or, cross the room, moving toward a specific focus but perform it as if some magic hand was editing, and you are alternatively a male and a female. Note: This is useful for identifying and breaking stereotypical movement patterns. Difficult. (Symbols)

Adult/Child
Similar to above, but with emphasis on differences in movement behavior at different ages. (Symbols)

Days of Knights and Ladies
(Suggested music: A pavane from the sixteenth century.) Imagine yourself slipping back into the time of Queen Elizabeth, knighthood, and gallantry. Using your arms and hands as an elegant decoration to your refined bearing, walk elegantly. Try tracing intricate floor patterns, executing them with pride. The weight of your clothes keeps your movements restrained, perhaps aloof. Although an exalted member of the court, above the servile underlings whom you command and who attend to your daily needs, you are gracious, acknowledging the people you pass with restraint and courtesy, possibly touching hands lightly or circling around and walking a pattern with them. Note: This improv concentrates on the solemnity and restraint of the royalty whose heavy garments restricted and thereby influenced their daily and dance movement, giving rise to the first of the court dance forms, the pavane: stately, slow, patterned, restrained. Use in Dance History class. (Self as Part of the Group; Movement and Movement Qualities; unit 8, Art Forms)

Hunger
Use the idea of food, hunger, and starvation for an improv drama. It may relate to current events or provoke personal responses: hunger becomes anger-driving-seeking distraction (dancing like crazy), or light-headedness, or sluggishness. It can also lead to feelings

connected with food, eating, dieting, body image. Note: This could be a heavy but potentially significant improv, especially because eating disorders such as bulemia and anorexia are so prevalent today. Be particularly sensitive when presenting it to certain populations (teenage girls, dancers). *(Smell and Taste)*

Cultural Heritage   See chapter 9, "Advanced Challenges."

Other Applicable Improvs (for page numbers see index)
Hiding
Faces
Gesture (use social gestures that imply a relation between people)
Postures (use pictures of people in social situations)
Becoming Civilized
Kinespheres
The Encounter
Conversation II
Supports
Confrontation
A Gift
Take Down
Poison
Elephant Game
Trading Focus (encourage the two groups to interact)
Rhythm Circle
Roar In
Impulse/Follow-through
Dictated Conversation
Getting Out I & II
Slow Changes
Line
Three Kinds of Movement
The Fool
Monsters
One Symbol, Three Approaches
Symbolic Costumes
Masks
The Sixties

Improv Ideas
initiations
rites of passage
the ages of man
martial arts: meditation and defense
societies' dictates (bound feet, veiled faces, shaven heads)
doing penance
war and peace
race
the contest
a birth
a death
a marriage
a divorce
welcome!
independence
jailed
the judgment
help!
in-laws
male bonding
parenting
as a child
the dictator
"of the people, by the people, . . . "
student/teacher
unrequited love
in mourning
at work
a feast
first date
in church (worship, the sermon, confession)
feeding
sharing food
the put down
the sting
the king, the queen, the court, and the fool
at play

the curse
victory/defeat
submission
position of authority
rally
debutante ball
women's work/men's work
the clown within
big business
mafia
the politicians
in the subways
macho
an escape
the sacrifice
the picnic
the afterworld
pilgrimage
burning candles
at prayer
the attack
stress
satire
sneers and snubs
the outcast
in defiance
the oldest profession
the pick-up
slow dancing
the smile
the kiss
the parade
sports
alone in a crowd
the matriarch
the snake pit
in the stocks
auction

"eat drink and be merry for . . . "
member of the gang
revival
one-upmanship
gambling
the goddesses: Hera, Athena, Demeter, Persephone, Aphrodite,
    Hecate
the gods: Zeus, Apollo, Dionysus, Mercury

Index

Note: Titles of improvs and the pages on which they are described are given in **boldface** type.